The Social Life of the Hebrews

I0125086

Rev. Edward Day

Routledge
Taylor & Francis Group

First published in 1901

This edition first published in 2011 by Routledge
4 Park Square, Milton Park, Abingdon, Oxon, OX14 4RN

Simultaneously published in the USA and Canada
by Routledge
605 Third Avenue, New York, NY 10017

Routledge is an imprint of the Taylor & Francis Group, an informa business

Publisher's Note
The publisher has gone to great lengths to ensure the quality of this
reprint but points out that some imperfections in the original copies may
be apparent.

Disclaimer
The publisher has made every effort to trace copyright holders and
welcomes correspondence from those they have been unable to contact.

A Library of Congress record exists under LC Control Number: 01030573

ISBN 13: 978-0-415-68161-2 (hbk)
ISBN 13: 978-0-203-80478-0 (ebk)

Routledge Revivals

The Social Life of the Hebrews

First published in 1901, this study of the social life of the Hebrews considers both the time of the judges and the time of the monarchy. Written in a popularly scientific style, designed to appeal to students of ancient Middle East and biblical history as well as the general reader, this work details the social life and history of allied Semitic races, covering the period of time from the settlement of Canaan to the breakup of the Northern Kingdom in 722 BC.

The Semitic Series

THE SOCIAL LIFE OF THE HEBREWS

BY THE

REV. EDWARD DAY

LONDON
JOHN C. NIMMO
14 KING WILLIAM STREET, STRAND
MDCCCCI

CONTENTS

PART I

THE TIME OF THE JUDGES

CHAPTER VII

CHAPTER VIII

CHAPTER IX

CHAPTER X

PART II

THE TIME OF THE MONARCHY

CHAPTER I

CHAPTER II

CHAPTER III

CHAPTER XII

CHAPTER XIII

APPENDIX

PART I

THE TIME OF THE JUDGES

THE SOCIAL LIFE OF THE HEBREWS

CHAPTER I

INTRODUCTION

THE designation of the period of Hebrew life which
is considered in this part of the present work is not
as easy as it at first thought seems, for the term here
employed, the usual one, is misleading, though perhaps not as misleading to many as some other might
be. The time covered is from the settlement of
Canaan to the monarchy. This was a period when
the Hebrews for the most part were wanting in unity,
when the clans grouped themselves in certain parts
of Canaan, revealing in some instances their kinship,
as in the case of the Leah and Rachel clans. If there
had been something akin to national life prior to the
settlement, during their nomadic wanderings, it must
have grown very largely out of the circumstances of
that life. When they entered Canaan, as there will
be an endeavour to show later, they went up in groups
to their various allotments or destinations and established themselves as best they could. Later, on
rare occasions, clan aided clan, and on occasions rarer
still, group or tribe aided some clan in extremity.
Not apparently until near the close of this period,
when the Philistines, more capable of united action

than the Canaanites, came into prominence and set
themselves to harry and to oppress the Hebrews, was
there developed and manifested some considerable
national spirit. The clans were then measurably
drawn together under Saul, the son of Kish,[1] who
stood at the parting of the ways, partaking of the
character of a local vindicator or deliverer. He prepared the way for David, in whom the monarchy really
had its origin.

The so-called Judges were necessarily limited in
influence, both as to territory and as to time. As
vindicators or deliverers their work was in each instance confined to a comparatively small section of
the land. When their work was done, though they
may not have sunk into obscurity, they ceased to
control or to rally and to lead. Judges they never
became in the popular understanding of the term.
Much, then, as we may object to the term, "the Time
of the Judges," on the grounds mentioned we still retain it.

Scholars are no longer able to accept the chronology of the Book of Judges. The figures given belong to the additions made to the texts by late redactors and are as unreliable as are the statements that
these different heroes individually ruled over all
Israel. Instead of a period of four hundred years,
we have but two hundred and fifty or three hundred years at most,[2] though we include the days of

---

[1] The extent to which Saul, and later the House of Saul, looked
to Benjamin for support is worthy of note.

[2] Budde gives as the approximate date of the Exodus, 1250 B.C.;
as the date of the invasion of Canaan, 1200; as that of the begin-

Samuel and Saul which present substantially the same type of social life.

But though we, after bringing this period down to the close of the life of Saul, shorten it as compared with the old chronology one hundred to one hundred and fifty years, we have to admit its importance. Not until the last few decades of Old Testament study in the light of the higher criticism gave us our true perspective were we able to understand the mighty import of those transitional, yet formative, years of early Hebrew life. During this period the Hebrews ceased to be a pastoral, and became an agricultural, people. That this necessitated a momentous change in their social life must be evident to all who are familiar with the two types of civilisation. Then there were the changes that came from contact with the Canaanites; and later those that grew out of the hostility and pressure of the Philistines.

The old view, according to which a monotheistic people, numbering several millions, passed into a land that of right was theirs, exterminating its inhabitants, and, save for occasional relapses, prospered and multiplied until they were ready for a king for whom they were so foolish as to ask, is discredited in the light which patient investigation has thrown upon the period. Instead of this we have various clans, containing at the most a few thousand each, making with all that it involved socially the mighty

ning of the monarchy under David, 1000. Kautzsch puts the Exodus earlier, as 1320 B.C. This brings the invasion into the early part of the thirteenth century B.C. Only in the latter date, the time of David, does he agree with Budde.

change from a nomadic to an agricultural life while at the same time changing radically their environment. During this period ideals and institutions were forming that later played an important part in the life of the people, while at the same time they were slowly drawn together as their interests became one in face of a common peril. Civilised they did not, in our modern acceptation of the term, become; far from it; but they made great strides in this direction and secured in so doing some intellectual and moral values that marked a decided advance in thought and religion.

This period, then, so important, is here studied as the earliest period, for back of it we can go but a little way. We may take it for granted that the Hebrews had lived in Egypt and had there felt the lash of the task-master. The statement of Dr. Budde in *The Religion of Israel to the Exile*, p. 10, is one which we can readily endorse: "The Israelites knew that their forefathers had been restored by the help of their God from Egyptian bondage to the freedom of the steppe, and thence led to their permanent abode. The witness of the historical documents to this fact does not stand alone. The earliest prophets presuppose it as an incontestable truth. It is inconceivable that a free people should have stamped on the memory of their ancestors the brand of a disgraceful servitude unless it had a foundation of historical truth. All that can be considered doubtful is whether it was the whole people of Israel that fell under the Egyptian bondage, or Joseph alone." Admitting all this, we still have to confess that we know next to nothing of the social life of the Hebrews during the time of their Egyptian sojourn ; but we may safely say that prior to their entering Canaan they had for a long time lived as nomads and that their life for centuries had presumably been essentially nomadic. It was probably as shepherds that they were known even in Egypt. But though they lived as nomads before entering Canaan, the records of their desert life are well nigh as scanty as those of the Egyptian period. Of authentic contemporary literature we have little. It is a well-known fact that the material in Exodus, Leviticus, and Numbers that professes to be contemporary is largely [1] exilic, while Deuteronomy belongs to the days of Josiah. With so little material at our disposal, it seems unwise to attempt to reconstruct the social life of that period in a separate part ; but it may be carefully studied in connection with the settlement of, and later life in, Canaan. By way of contrast the old life may in its more distinctive features be brought out while dwelling upon the settled, agricultural life, thus adding to the interest of the story of the social life in the time of the Judges.

That the years, whether forty or more, passed in the desert were important in their influence upon the Hebrew clans, we must admit. Socially, if not industrially, there must have been changes ; but morally and religiously the development must have been still more marked. Whether the Hebrews had known God as one and as Yahweh prior to the Exodus, or

[1] Not wholly, for the J and E narratives as found in Exodus and Numbers treat the period imaginatively.

whether, as Budde has so ably argued, they through Moses accepted Yahweh,[1] the God of the Kenites, as their God, they surely emerged from their desert life as the people of Yahweh. Up to this time the world had probably not seen a loftier conception of the Divine Being. It took centuries of thought for the Hebrews to fill this concept with the rich content which appears in the teaching of Amos and Hosea, to say nothing of Isaiah and Deutero-Isaiah ; but even then, at the time of the settlement, there was a purity and an elevation in their thought of their God that could have been found only in the deity of a nomadic people, and that, too, a people peculiarly cir-cumstanced. By bringing out, therefore, the distin-guishing traits of the social life of the people while nomads, in depicting the social life of the time of the Judges, the writer presents the first of two parts on the social life of the Hebrew people ; so that, as it lies in his own mind, the designation, "the Social Life of the Early Hebrews," is the appropriate title for this part, though for reasons above suggested he retains the phrase, "the Time of the Judges."

It will be found necessary in the progress of this work to make frequent reference to sources from which data have been obtained, as it will to cite mod-ern authorities that corroborate the author in the positions taken. As the text of such a work cannot

[1] *The Religion of Israel to the Exile.* As this is a prominent contention of the earlier chapters of this volume, these American lectures should be carefully read by the student who would under-stand the question of the origin of Yahwism. (Cf. also Cornill, *The Prophets of Israel*, 3d ed., p. 20, f.—CR.)

be overloaded with critical discussions or explanations, the foot-notes must necessarily be ample, for the questions which will occur to the reader, unless he has himself worked these same sources critically, will have to do with the data upon which statements are based. The author may have had ample historical and sociological warrant for his assertions, but if he refers to such data it must be in the way of foot-notes or appendix; and he must make such references frequently, because, otherwise, his statements would put altogether too much strain upon the credulity of the reader.

The student of the social life of this period finds at his disposal a large body of sociological data embedded in folk-lore and song. These data, though invaluable, need to be very carefully handled that the real and indisputable facts may be made to appear. Such student finds also considerable historical material in the original sources, though very little that belongs to the age itself. Much of the Book of Judges is the work of late redactors and has consequently little value for our present constructive work, while some of it belongs to the priestly writers of the exilic period and has still less value. It is a fact that must be recognised, apt as some are to scout the thought, that the student of to-day, with his knowledge of early Semitic life and his critical apparatus, is better able to reconstruct the social life of the period under consideration than was the Priestly Writer seven hundred years after the settlement, or the Deuteronomist four hundred years after. To have lived five centuries before Christ, or even eight cen-

turies before, did not necessarily render the Hebrew
writer infallible as to the early life of his people.
Traditions there undoubtedly were in abundance, but
time had wrought changes in them; ample written
material there must have been, though such material
must have passed through strange vicissitudes. If
Deuteronomist and Priestly Writer had not worked
over this material in Joshua, for example, from their
own peculiar point of view, we might have much more
trustworthy data than we have; as it is, we are forced
to ignore for our purposes almost the whole of it.
Yet the Book of Joshua, as we have it, is not by any
means without value to the historical and sociological
student, for there are portions that admirably supplement the oldest portions of the Book of Judges.

But just what, it is here profitable to inquire, have
we as reliable data in Joshua, Judges, and 1 Samuel?
We have the fragmentary story of the settlement
found in Judges, chap. i., omitting the several additions of the redactor, as the reference to the death
of Joshua, v. 1, the reference to the conquest of
Canaanites and Perizzites, v. 4, the statement concerning the capture of Jerusalem, v. 8, and that as
to the capture of Gaza, Askelon, and Ekron, v. 18,
etc.[1] With this chapter of Judges we should compare certain fragments from the same ancient sources
preserved in the Book of Joshua, xiii. 13; xv. 14–19;
xv. 63; xvi. 10; xvii. 11–18; xix. 47.[2] Very curious
are these passages embedded in the text of Joshua,
so utterly at variance are they with the bulk of
that work. The second chapter of Judges informs

[1] See Appendix I.　　　　[2] Cf. here the Septuagint.

us that the Messenger of Yahweh (the allusion is probably to the Ark which was carried) went up from Gilgal to Bethel, that there the people offered sacrifice unto Yahweh; it tells us also that Yahweh left the people, that is, the Canaanites, not dispossessing them at once; that the Israelites dwelt in the midst of them, intermarried with them and served their gods. Aside from this the chapter is late. The story of Ehud, Judges iii. 15-28, must be considered trustworthy; so, too, must the great battle ode of Judges v. Just what the story of the overthrow of the Canaanites in chap. iv. has for our purposes it is hard to say. As a parallel to the Song of Deborah it is inferior and unreliable. Probably there was a story of the overthrow of Jabin of Hazor (see Joshua xi.), but it is here so mutilated in the endeavour to bring it into harmony with the later campaign against Sisera, as to be of no great use to us. Joshua, chap. xi., may be more reliable, though the text bears marks of being worked over. The folk-story of Gideon, embedded in Judges, vi.-viii., in its oldest form, which, as used by us, is very simple in outline, is invaluable, but it needs to be studied in Moore's *Polychrome Judges* or in connection with Driver's *Introduction to the Literature of the Old Testament* to be understood by the average reader. The Abimelech story, so far as it has to do with Gaal ben Obed, ix. 26-41, bears the marks of extreme antiquity; of the remainder there are portions that contain sociological data of great value. The same may be said of the Jephthah story, xi., xii. Critical scholars are inclined to accept the Samson story, as given in chap-

ters xiii.–xvi., with few alterations.[1] The story of
Micah's idols and of the migration of the Danites,
xvii., xviii., received many a touch by later hand, but
it bears the marks in the main of a contemporary narrator. Not so much can be said of the story of the
outrage of Gibeah, xix.–xxi., for it is dual in form,
yet even here there are valuable sociological data.

1 Samuel should not be neglected, but if used it
should be with such critical guides as Driver's *Introduction to the Literature of the Old Testament* and
Smith's *Samuel*, in *The International Critical Commentary*. The need of criticism of the text is more
imperative here than in the case of the Judges, because it has suffered more. See especially passages
in which Samuel figures prominently as judge and
theocratic leader. The story of Saul's career as it
comes out in 1 Samuel ix. 1–10, 16 ; xi. 1–11, 15 ; xiii.
and xiv., also the Saul and David stories, with allow-
ances for reduplications, etc., save xix. 18–24 and a
few other passages, should be studied.[2]

[1] These stories are of great value from the social point of view,
and have historical value as well (in opposition to the solar-myth
theory), yet it must be said that myth and legend are no less dis-
tinguishable than the historic element.—CR.

[2] The leading English and American authorities accessible to the
reader should be named, for he who tries to master the original
sources without them labours at a great disadvantage. W. H. Bennett's *Joshua*, in *The English Polychrome* of *The Sacred Books of the
Old Testament ;* G. F. Moore's *Judges*, in *The English Polychrome*
and in *The International Critical Commentary ;* and Driver's *Introduction to the Literature of the Old Testament* are indispensable.
Among other works that help one to understand early Hebrew life
are W. Robertson Smith's *Kinship and Marriage* and his *The Religion of the Semites ;* H. C. Trumbull's three volumes : *The Blood Cov-*

The authorities named may suggest to the reader a preference for the works of the higher critics. It is, perhaps, enough to say frankly that the reader is not wrong in his surmise. The student who seeks to master the social life of this very obscure and difficult period without these illuminative guides, sets himself to a hopeless task. Only men thoroughly imbued with the modern historico-critical spirit are able to open up to us intelligently in Old Testament study the original sources. All difficulties do not vanish under their leadership, but the worst and the most perplexing do ; besides, they lift from the back of faith by their critical separation and elucidation of the texts many a burden which faith should never be made to bear. A study of the social life of the time between the settlement of Canaan and the monarchy should not follow the lines laid down in the general histories. More and other data must be brought together, and such data must be looked at throughout from the social point of view. This point of view largely determines the particular topics treated and the order in which they are taken up.

enant, *The Threshold Covenant*, and *The Covenant of Salt ;* Tiele's *The Science of Religion ;* and Tylor's *Primitive Culture* and kindred studies in anthropology. Besides these textual and other works named, may be mentioned several authorities of great value often referred to in these pages : Budde's *The Religion of Israel to the Exile ;* Piepenbring's *Histoire du Peuple d'Israël ;* Kittel's *History of the Hebrews ;* Wellhausen's article *Israel* in the *Encyclopædia Britannica ;* Kautzsch's *The Literature of the Old Testament*, and G. A. Smith's *Historical Geography of the Holy Land.* Hastings' *Dictionary of the Bible* and Cheyne and Black's *Encyclopædia Biblica* are of exceptional value upon the topics connected with this period.

In this Part I., the environment, geographical and ethnographical, in so far as it affected the social life of the period is first considered. The clan is then studied as the primitive form of social organisation, and its influence upon the life of the people noted. Next, the family as a social organism of growing importance is taken up. This chapter is in turn followed by one on the social significance of sacrifice. The influence of individuals upon the social life is considered at length. Industry, trade, and travel, as they had to do with the same aspects of that life, receive attention. Some stories characteristic of the time are carefully studied. The character of the religion of the people and its importance as a social factor precedes a chapter on the transition in the direction of national unity toward the close of the period.

CHAPTER II

THE ENVIRONMENT

WE have to do with a people fixed to the land upon which they lived. The social life of the Hebrews after they settled in Canaan was not what it had been anterior to the settlement. Little is known of them up to this time. The fragmentary and imperfect records that remain in what purports to be a history of their progenitors in Genesis, and in later portions of the Hexateuch of themselves while in Egypt and after they got out into the Arabian peninsula, when freed from the manifest marks of late prophetic and priestly historians, leave us in great uncertainty. But that they were a nomadic people beyond the Jordan, before they entered Canaan, living as shepherds or herdsmen, unsettled and migratory, without private property in land, cultivating the ground but little if at all, subsisting for the most part upon their flocks and herds, with customs that differed not materially from those of later nomads of Arabia, is indisputable. That this old social order very largely disappeared,[1] giving place slowly in some regions, more rapidly in others, as they with considerable difficulty crowded in and took possession of unoccupied regions,[2] or dispos-

[1] Kittel, *His. of the Heb.*, vol. ii., p. 93; Hastings' *Dict. of the Bib.*, vol. ii., p. 807 ff.

[2] Budde, *Rel. of Is. to the Ex.*, p. 48 ff. ; cf. Ex. xxiii. 29, 30, with Judges ii. 23a; iii. 2.

sessed some of the weaker hill-folk west of the Jordan, we must also believe. They became an agricultural people, having homes of their own in villages and cities, though still to a considerable extent clinging to their flocks, practising not only the art of husbandry but also those closely allied thereto, the making of wine, oil, etc.

In this chapter we are interested in the environment of their new social life, physical, intellectual, and spiritual. The various clans in three main and practically independent divisions or movements pushed up from the plain of the Jordan where, near Gilgal and Jericho which had fallen into their hands, they had lived for some time after crossing the river. One company made its way up into the hill country of the south, another, consisting of two large and two small clans, secured the highlands of Central Canaan, the third, with little show of conquest, advanced into the hill country of the north. Beginning with the south and passing to the extreme north, we shall sketch, as far as our imperfect data enable us, the ethnographical and geographical environment of the different clans.[1]

Western Palestine had for centuries upon its south the Edomites and the Amalekites. With the former, according to apparently authentic tradition, the Hebrews were allied in race but at times involved in war. This need not seem strange, for the Edomites inhabited a rocky, and for the most part barren territory, and therefore depended largely upon

---

[1] For a harmony of passages relating to the settlement, see Appendix I. For Philistines, Appendix III.; for Hittite, IV.; for Amorites, V.

the plunder of caravans for a subsistence. With
the latter there was perpetual enmity and hostility. Farther up we find upon our left hand the
small clan of Simeon living in close relations with
another and stronger Leah clan, that of Judah. To
our right and still farther on we find the Kenites and
the Calebites. The Kenites were perhaps a clan of the
Amalekites inhabiting the wilderness of Judea, and,
unlike their parent clan, on most friendly terms as a
semi-nomadic people with Judah and his other allied
clans. The Calebites, apparently a clan of the Edomites, settled in Hebron and the country to the south
thereof. The friendly terms upon which the Kenites
lived with Israel appears in the tradition which is a
part of the J document of the Hexateuch that Hobab
was Moses' father-in-law ; just as the friendly relations subsisting between Midian and Israel at an
earlier time found expression in E and D in the tradition that Jethro of Midian was father-in-law of
Moses.[1] In the region north of that occupied by the
clan of Caleb we come upon the clan of Judah holding the highlands of Southern Canaan, with, probably,
such towns as Tekoah, Bethlehem, and Succoth in
their hands, but not the city of Jerusalem,[2] which to
the time of David was held by the Jebusites, and
not the cities of Kirjath-Jearim, Aijalon, and Gibeon
to the northwest. In a narrow and unfertile region
to the northeast of Jerusalem we find the clan of
Benjamin, closely affiliated with the clans of Joseph

[1] Moore, *Judges, I. C.*, pp. 32, 33 ; Budde, *Rel. of Is. to the Ex.*,
pp. 19–23.

[2] Josh. **xv**. 63 ; 2 Samuel v. 6–9 ; Judges i. 8, 21.

as a part of an older clan, that of Rachel. North of
Beth-shemesh, then and long after a Canaanite city,
and south of the vale of Aijalon, occupying the towns
of Eshtaol and Zorah and the immediately contiguous
country, we find the little clan of Dan of the Bilhah-
Rachel clan or group, and so on friendly terms with
its near neighbour Ephraim. Before the days of the
Judges pass we shall see this clan, or the larger part
of it, six hundred men with their wives and children,
disheartened by the pressure of the Canaanites, who
would not allow them to spread out in the plain below toward the Mediterranean, making their way to
a beautiful and fertile region at the sources of the
Jordan.[1] The extent of the hill territory held by
the great clans of Ephraim and Manasseh, and the
fact that Ephraim had within or near its limits the
old sanctuaries of Bethel and Shiloh, as well as the
more important Canaanite sanctuary of Shechem,
which was in the centre of Ephraim though not under the control of the Ephraimites, as well as the numerical superiority of these Joseph clans, give the
central part of Canaan peculiar interest. If Judah
seems the more important because of its history
for two centuries prior to the Captivity, as also
because of its history subsequent thereto, we need to
remember that at this time it was relatively, as compared with the other prominent clans, a much smaller
clan, possessing a much smaller territory and considerably isolated, because separated from the clans of
Joseph by a Canaanite region with strongly fortified

[1] Smith, *His. Geo. Holy Land*, pp. 220, 473, 480 f.   Cheyne and
Black, *Encyc. Bib.*, vol. i., c. 992 ff.

cities. The clans of Joseph had to content themselves
with their highlands. Cities on their border and in
the plain below them easily held their own for centuries, keeping even their dependencies out of the
hands of these invaders. From Beth-shean and her
dependencies, passing through Ibleam, Taanach, and
Megiddo, with their dependencies, to Dor upon the
Mediterranean, south of Carmel, was a line of strong
Canaanite centres that remained unsubjugated until
the time of David, and that continued to be predomi-
natingly heathen until long after.[1] These cities were
strategic ones situated in or near the great plain of
Esdraelon. Peopled as they were by the native Canaanites, they separated the third section of Israel
from the remainder.

The northern clans need not long detain us. They
still more imperfectly seized the land whither they
went, that known later as lower and upper Galilee,
as the stronger clans elected to make homes for themselves in Central and Southern Canaan. Issachar
settled between the great plain and the lake of Galilee, not far from the clan of Manasseh. Zebulun
fixed upon the territory to the north of the plain and
Issachar. Asher, as a clan, settled still farther to the
north and west, endeavouring to work his way down
to the seaside while holding on to what he was able to
secure of the West Lebanon region; Naphtali settled
to the right, in a region stretching off toward the sea
of Galilee. This fertile region of the well-watered

[1] Judges i. 27 ; Moore, *Judges, P.,* p. 50. (Here and elsewhere
P. is used for the *English Polychrome* as *I. C.* is for the *Interna
tional Critical Commentary.*)

hills of Galilee, thus partially occupied by this third wave or migration, was so imperfectly secured that even after their victories over Jabin and Sisera these northern clans seem to have largely lost themselves through mingling with the Canaanites, so that they played a subordinate part in the later history of Israel. The unimportant clans of Reuben and Gad[1] to the east of the Jordan will find small place in our study.

It is thus evident that the territory possessed by these clans of nomads for several centuries after they had left behind them their nomadic life was small. Save perhaps in the case of Ephraim, it was to a considerable extent Canaanitish, while all about and among these Israelites were Canaanites, a Semitic people like themselves and much further advanced in the arts of life as town dwellers and agriculturalists than they were. There had been some fighting, as there was to be more, but for the most part the settlement (we refuse to use the term conquest here) had been bloodless, not because the Israelites, being fearless, independent men of the desert were less warlike, but rather because the Canaanites were so much more numerous and so much further advanced in the arts of life, as was seen in their well-fortified cities. In another direction the Canaanites had the advantage of the Hebrews; they, at least those inhabiting the cities of the plains, had horses and chariots of war. The Hebrew clans had neither. Only to a very limited extent then was there a conquest. Self-invited, the Hebrews as Semitic desert clans pressed

[1] Hastings' *Dictionary*, vol. ii., p. 76 ff.

in, and took up their abode among the hills in regions
that the agricultural Canaanites had probably left
unsettled. They needed not an extensive territory,
for they were not great in point of numbers. The
40,000 mentioned in the Song of Deborah probably
included most of the fighting men of Israel at the
time. The territory they needed they appear to have
secured without much bloodshed.

We have ceased to extenuate the stories of the
slaughter of the Canaanites found in the Book of
Joshua and elsewhere, because we now know that
there were no such pitilessly cruel wars.[1] The
stories of the two campaigns attributed to Joshua,
which, according to the accounts of them, exterminated the Canaanites and gave Israel an unoccupied
stage upon which to play his part, are irreconcilable
with the history of the time of the Judges, when the
Canaanites are so superior in numbers to the Hebrews.

Outside of Canaan were the Amalekites, the Midianites, and other nomadic peoples of the desert to
the south and east to trouble them as they multiplied
and increased in importance. Even the Moabites
and Ammonites across the Jordan, in East Palestine,
were to imperil them, while later, at the close of
the period considered, the Philistines were to establish themselves in the western plain and, spreading
forth as an enterprising and fairly well civilised and
warlike people, were to harass them and leave them
at the time of the formation of the kingdom under

[1] Hastings' *Dictionary*, vol. ii., p. 807 ; Piepenbring, *His. du
Peu. d'Is.*, p. 69 ff.

Saul greatly disorganised, tribally and socially.   The great Hittite power on the north, which perhaps because of its might as compared with this feeble folk, could afford to do so, was for the most part to ignore them.   If there were invasions of the Hittites during this period, the Canaanites probably suffered far more than the Hebrews.   That there was a great movement on the part of Egypt against the Hittites, in which the Egyptians were successful, seems clear, but that the Hebrews suffered comparatively little, seems also probable.   Though they were poorly organised and to a considerable extent unable to protect themselves, this period of their history must have been, on the whole, one of expansion and normal growth.

The climate of Palestine, owing to the salubrious breezes both from the western sea and from the northern mountains, made it possible for the Israelites to develop among the hills which they occupied a healthy physique.   George Adam Smith has pointed out, however, that the Deuteronomist was right, when several centuries later he reminded his people that there was no inevitableness about their land, as in the case of Egypt;[1] that it taught them their providential dependence upon their God, to whom as labourers or agriculturalists they must look for such climatic conditions as insured success.

Though undoubtedly inferior morally, the Canaanites were certainly intellectually and industrially the superior of the Israelites.[2]   In contact with the Hit-

[1] Deut. xi. ; Geo. A. Smith, *His. Geo. of the H. L.*, p. 73 f.

[2] Hastings' *Dictionary*, vol. ii., p. 510; Budde, *Rel. of Is. to Ex.*, pp. 11, 55 ; Kittel, *His. of Heb.*, vol. ii., p. 94.

tites on the north and with Egypt on the southwest, and moulded as they were by the learning and culture of Babylonia on the east, while they were allied to, and in close industrial relation with, the enterprising Phœnicians of the northwest, the Canaanites were able to influence strongly these men of the desert, who must have looked up to them and have shown an eagerness to learn of them. The contact of these Hebrew clans with the Canaanites was far from being an unmitigated evil.

This, then, was the environment of these clans which according to tradition passed with Joshua over the Jordan; and this we shall find was to make its influence felt in determining the arts, the customs, and to some extent, possibly to a great extent, the religion, if not well nigh the whole life of this most interesting people.

CHAPTER III

THE CLAN

MORE important than the family as a social organism in primitive times among the Semites, in its influence upon and its power over life, was the clan. Despite the position taken by the great anthropologists and sociologists of two or three decades ago, we are coming, under the guidance of later investigators, to see that primitive man was dominated very largely by the clan, while the family in its influence upon him played a subordinate part. The clan as an organisation seems to have antedated the family. Primitive man probably lived under a matriarchate.[1] Kinship was constituted by uterine ties, and descent was reckoned through female lines, the father's relation to his children being ignored. Traces of this origin of the Hebrew clan may be seen in the fact that the harlot had apparently some social position, and in such names as Leah, Rachel, Zilpah, and Bilhah, which among the Hebrews were apparently clan names. What are called the *sadiqa* marriages of the period of the Judges point in the same direction. A study of early Arabian life, though such study cannot by any means take us back to the time under consideration, may be regarded as revealing not only the conditions

[1] Appendix II.

24

that existed in the centuries immediately antedating Mohammed, but also with tolerable accuracy the conditions for many centuries anterior thereto. It points in the same direction. In those times, as Robertson Smith has shown, the family was subordinate to the clan. Industry, religion, marriage, and nearly the whole social life of the people, came under the surveillance of the clan. Property rights were vested in the clan, and only the clan had any legal existence practically. A man might marry without the clan only upon such terms as the clan might permit by its customs or by its action in a particular case; a woman might be allowed, where compensation was made, to marry and leave her clan, or she might contract through father or other male relative with a man of another clan, a *sadiqa* union or marriage,[1] and so remain with her people and bear children for her clan. Unmistakable traces of such unions of members of different clans are found in the old folk-lore tales of the Book of Judges. Jerubbaal contracted, according to story, a *sadiqa* alliance with a Canaanite woman of Shechem, to whom Abimelech was born.[2] As the fruit of such a marriage Abimelech was supposed to belong to the Shechemites. He took advantage of this fact in seeking to win over the men of Shechem. The Samson story in its simplest form is probably very old. In it the Canaanites of the plain southwest of the vale of Aijalon, in or near which dwelt the clan of Dan, must have figured rather than the Philistines, who later came into this region. This semi-mythical

[1] W. R. Smith, *Kin. and Mar.*
[2] Judges viii. 31; ix. 1 ff. ; Moore, *Judges, I. C.*, pp. 235 ff., 340.

Danite is said to have contracted with a woman of Timnath such an alliance, which was not, however, maintained because of her breach of faith in giving to the Timnathites the answer to his riddle.   In the same way, though marriage was usually between members of the same clan, unions may have been formed between members of the different clans among the Hebrews themselves.   This seems the more likely from the fact that among these clans, as among the Arabs at a much later day, there were women who as harlots received into their tents or dwellings men of other clans and were not looked upon with disfavour, because they bore children to their clans.   The strength of the family tie among the early Hebrews as known to us may be admitted in spite of the predominance of the clan even at this time.   Never apparently among the Hebrews was the family tie as loose as in Arabia, where the husband would put a favourite wife with her tent at the disposal of his guest.[1] But despite the growing importance of the family the clan at the time of the settlement had great importance in their eyes, and life was lived chiefly with a view to its aggrandisement.   As the clan developed it became incorporated in great tribes, and the family, as the tribe increased in size, became of more importance as a social organisation, but even then new clans were formed within the tribal group, and others incorporated from without.

[1] This custom is said to have held among the Arabs to within the present century.   Probably, in most instances, an honorarium was expected of the guest who had made such use of a wife's tent ; but it appears not to have been always.

So important was a man's standing in his clan that if he was cast out he perforce became an outlaw, unless, indeed, some clan could be found to receive him. This seems to have been the case with Jephthah who, being cast out of his own clan, probably not because he was the son of a harlot, for that would not have imperilled his standing, but for other reasons, got together a lot of rough and lawless men, as David did later under similar circumstances, and lived a life of outlawry in the land of Tob. After the settlement of Canaan the clan must have changed somewhat, if, indeed, it did not slowly degenerate as an organisation. Hostile influences were probably at work tending to transform it, but the disorganised condition of society must, at times, in some ways, have increased the allegiance of members to their clan.

These different clans had their chiefs or leaders; probably they had compact and easily working civil and military organisations. In the Song of Deborah there is an allusion to Reuben that has been thought to refer not without reason to something akin to an assembly of proprietors, or freemen, who discussed the question of joining Issachar, Zebulun, and other northern clans in a campaign against Sisera. These, however, being too far away to be greatly interested personally, let the time pass in indecisive talk, and failed to respond. This was probably a communal or clan assembly of freemen.

Some clans at the time of the settlement seem to have been disorganised, some to have been broken up and wholly or partially incorporated with other clans. The story found in Judges xx. and xxi. which relates an experience in which the clan of Benjamin was shattered, must have back of it a kernel of truth. In some way the neighbouring clans seem to have been incensed against Benjamin, because, it may be, that clan claimed or sought the hegemony. The Shechem story recorded in Genesis xxxiv., which appears to have as its basis the story of the violating of the Canaanite sanctuary at that place, may account for the broken condition of Simeon and Levi;[1] the latter losing in some way, as the history of the time reveals, its organisation as a clan, the former playing, as the same history shows, but a subordinate part in the actual life of Israel. None of the folk-lore tales of the Hebrews is more puzzling than this old Genesis story. In the fragmentary form in which it has been preserved, the sons of Jacob appear in an unenviable light, though of the two widely divergent forms of the narrative which are interwoven, one relieves the Israelites somewhat from blame by presenting an excuse for the massacre that might reasonably be pled in these rough times.

A daughter of the patriarch Jacob, according to one of the narratives, is taken by Shechem, the son of Hamor, and robbed of her virginal purity.[2] While

[1] Kittel, *His. of the Heb.*, vol. ii., pp. 69, 70; Budde, *Rel. of Is. to Ex.*, pp. 82 f., 84 ff. ; *Encyc. Brit.*, vol. xiii., p. 400; vol. xiv., p. 487; vol. xxii., p. 77; Moore, *Judges, I. C.*, pp. 35-37, etc.; Dillmann, *Genesis*, vol. ii., p. 287 ff.

[2] This is the J version of the story, while the one given later is according to E. Bacon, *Gen. of Gen.*, p. 177 ff.; cf. Dillmann, *Genesis*, here. It should here be remarked that J, or the Jehovistic narrative, usually regarded as originating in Judah, and E, or the Elohist, usually supposed to have originated in Ephraim, and P, or the

still detaining her in the city, Shechem comes to have a real fondness for her. " His soul," in the forceful words of the old chronicler, " cleaves to her." Jacob and his sons are highly incensed over the outrage, but they hold their peace, and, later when Shechem seeks to make her his by marriage, promising in addition to his bridal present to the girl a rich gift to them, be the price they please to set upon her what it may, if only she can be made his lawful wife, they gladly acquiesce, because of his delight in the girl and because of his high position among the sons of Hamor. It is not until afterward that there is treachery, and then only on the part of Simeon and Levi, sons of Jacob by Leah. They go forth and slay, not the inhabitants of the city, but Shechem and his father, and bring forth their sister, together with the spoil of the House of Hamor. Though nothing is done to them, they are rebuked by the father, who is not so much incensed against them because of their perfidy as he is made fearful lest he and his household, being "made to stink among the inhabitants of the land," may be exterminated. But their excuse that Shechem had dealt with their sister as with a harlot stops the mouth of the patriarch.

Curiously interwoven with this story is another which reflects more favourably the feeling which the violation of the city of Shechem engendered, though the blame of it is not, for some unaccountable reason,

Priestly narrative, were the great sources from which our Hexateuch, the first six books of our Bible, Judges and Samuel were very largely compiled.

put upon the two sons or clans alone. According to this narrative, which belongs to the Ephraimite history of early Israel as the other belongs to the Judahite, the daughter of the patriarch, urged by curiosity, goes forth to see her neighbour's daughters. She is seen by Shechem, who is at once attracted and speaks kindly to her. Afterward, in accordance with the custom of the early Semites, he begs his father to get the damsel as his wife. The father visits the sons of Jacob in order to establish a friendly covenant between them which shall permit intermarriage and the right of habitation and trade with the Israelites. The Israelites refuse, because the Hamorites are uncircumcised. Only upon condition that they be circumcised will they accede. The word which is carried back to the city by Hamor pleases the Shechemites, as it does his son. But having submitted to the rite, they are, while still physically incapacitated, set upon by the sons of Jacob, who slay them and make spoil of their city, carrying off their flocks and herds and asses, as well as what was in the city and in the country, together with their wives and little ones.[1]

A fragmentary and imperfect folk-lore tale is this, containing, as does the Judahite story, a basis of fact. We may be reasonably sure that Shechem was taken and spoiled by the clans of Simeon and Levi. That it was so may be seen in a stanza from one of the most ancient of Israel's poetic fragments, which belongs probably to the period of the early part of the monarchy in the ninth or tenth century B.C.

[1] For patriarchal stories of Genesis see Appendix VII.

Simeon and Levi are brethren;
Weapons of violence are their swords.
O my soul, come not thou into their council;
Unto their assembly, my glory, be not thou united;
For in their anger they slew a man,
And in their selfwill they houghed an ox.
Cursed be their anger, for it was fierce;
And their wrath, for it was cruel;
I will divide them in Jacob,
And scatter them in Israel.[1]

It does not require a severely trained critical sense
to discover in this impassioned poetry the terrible in-
dignation with which certain of the Hebrew clans regarded some impious deeds of treachery by the clans
of Simeon and Levi.   Whatever one may think of this
story and of the selection quoted from the Blessing of
Jacob[2] herewith given, he can hardly fail to notice
the small part taken by Simeon in the history of the
time, as he cannot fail to see that the Levites appear
during the period of the Judges without any semblance of tribal life.   All this, however, should not
lead us to overlook more important data.   The noteworthy thing which the early literature of the Hebrews brings out is that several of their clans had
a compact and workable organisation, and one so self-
sufficient that they were able to maintain themselves
and make their influence felt upon their members for
centuries.

[1] Gen. xlix. 5–7.   [2] Gen. xlix. 2–27.

CHAPTER IV

THE FAMILY

THE most interesting social institution among these clans, and the one that promised most for the future of Israel, was the family.[1] Though subordinate to the clan in many respects, it was destined to grow in importance. As the clans became larger and more unwieldy, and as they were slowly drawn nearer and nearer into something akin to a national life, the family acquired a self-sufficiency and local importance it had not hitherto possessed.

In a study of the social life of the Hebrews of any period of their history, the question concerning woman's position is a vital one. Though inferior at this time to what it was later, it was one of considerable importance. There is probably little literary material in the old Hebrew Scriptures that is older than the so-called Song of Deborah. It bears the marks of having been written at or near the time of the overthrow of Sisera by the northern clans, though it probably was not the work of Deborah herself. It reveals the fact that this remarkable woman was able to play a conspicuous part in that conflict. The passage which represents her as being of the clan of Ephraim,

[1] Hastings' *Dictionary*, vol. i., p. 846 ff.; Kittel, *His. of Heb.*, vol. ii., p. 298 f.

as residing under the palm-tree of Deborah near Bethel, and as judging Israel many years, is unreliable; but that this woman did incite and vindicate Israel, much as did the other Judges, seems evident. That in those troublous, turbulent times a woman could gain so much influence, thus making for herself a name that was celebrated in the songs of her people, is significant. The place assigned to the wife of Manoah in the old folk-tale of Samson and that occupied by Hannah in the later story of Samuel is suggestive of woman's position. It is the woman who first receives an intimation of the birth of a child who is to be devoted to Yahweh. And when she takes her husband into confidence, it is the woman who is again approached by the Messenger of Yahweh. Samson, upon reaching a marriageable age, communes with both his father and his mother. They are requested to get the young woman of Timnath for him. The father, as the party that must make all marriage-contracts for his sons, unless this is done by the clan, replies and refuses the request; but later at the wedding when the hero of the tale speaks to the young woman of the riddle, he assures her that he has not taken his father and mother into confidence. The writer leaves us to infer that had he told anyone he would have told his parents. The tradition concerning Abimelech's death discloses the fact that women were wont to bear a part in defensive warfare, as we know they did in industrial affairs. In this instance the woman adroitly dropped a heavy millstone so that it fractured the man's skull, though curiously enough without depriving him of consciousness.

The story of Jephthah's rash vow and of his immo-
lation of his daughter, so often likened to the touch-
ingly beautiful Greek story of Iphigenia, to which it is
in some respects superior, may be considered a plau-
sible folk-lore tale based upon facts in substantial
accord with it as it has come down to us.   Here
though the vow is regarded as irrevocable, the
daughter is made a party to the anguished father's
awful dilemma, and is permitted to reply : " My
father, thou hast spoken a solemn word to Yahweh ;
do to me as thou hast vowed, forasmuch as Yahweh
hath wrought for thee vengeance on thy foes."   The
father then, at her request, allows her to retire to the
mountains to bewail her sad fate with her mates.
There is no suggestion here of maidenhood as restrained and cloistered.

In the story of Benjamin's rape of the maidens of
Shiloh, the Canaanite inhabitants of which had sworn
not to intermarry their daughters with the shattered
clan of Benjamin, it is the same.   At the joyous
feast of the vintage the maidens, who had apparently
wrought with the young men in gathering and treading the grapes, come out of the city to join in the religious dances.   It is said of Samson that he saw
and talked with the Timnath girl he wished to marry,
and thus became enamoured of her.   The same freedom seems to have been accorded young women in
Israel.   Such stories as we find in the earlier portions of the Hexateuch, of the interview of Isaac's
servant with Rebekah, of Jacob with Rachel, and of
Moses with the daughters of Midian, though as literary compositions much later than the folk-stories

of the Judges, may be taken as reflecting a tolerably accurate conception of life as early as the period of the Judges.

Some qualifications need, however, to be made to what has been said about the high social position of woman among these Israelitish clans, for it seems evident that women, with all their freedom and social influence and independence, under certain circumstances were yet regarded as the chattels of the husband, the father, the brother, or of the clan. This seems true, not alone of concubines, as appears in the story of the outrage of Gibeah, where the father shows a willingness to sacrifice his virgin daughter rather than violate the sanctities of hospitality, but of women generally. The Book of the Covenant protects the virgin who has been violated, but it does so in the thought that she is the property of her father. A true conception of woman's worth and dignity was wanting. There was not that chivalrous treatment of woman that we might expect. Judges xix. 24 may be a reflection from Genesis xix. 8, though there are some reasons for supposing the Genesis story to be the later of the two. In either case we discover a want of chivalry in the regard for women in early Israel, and a failure to recognise her inviolable sanctity. This appears even more clearly in stories that at least reflect very early conceptions, though probably somewhat posterior to the time of the Judges. The three stories in Genesis, in two of which Abraham plays a leading part, and in one of which Isaac figures, may have had a common original, and that may have been late, but it is in evidence. An honored

progenitor of Israel is thought of as willing to imperil
his wife's chastity to save himself, and his wife is
thought of as submissively acquiescing.[1]

Woman appears to have borne more than her share
of the burdens of life. The work in and about the
home devolved upon her, even to the pitching of the
tent when they lived therein; she also shared in the
work of the field with the men at certain seasons.
The duties within the home must have been numerous,
as most of the material worn was made at home;
though whether the richly dyed stuffs and the embroidery referred to in Judges v. 30 were of home
manufacture may be questioned. The caravans which
frequently passed through the land brought the manufactured products of Damascus and Tyre to the door
of many a peasant, while the women shared in the
spoils of war, receiving as their perquisites all articles
of female apparel taken.

In thus dwelling upon woman we have made evident to a considerable extent the place of her husband
in the family. It remains to notice two directions in
which his superiority was especially marked. The re-
sponsibility for the care and the training of the children, at least after they had reached a certain age,
devolved upon him. Then he, as the head of the
family, was the priest offering the sacrifices which
necessarily appertained to all slaughter of domestic

[1] "The ancient Hebrews were far from possessing the chivalrous
feeling which we find among the old Arabs."—Moore, *Judges, I. C.*,
p. 418. The reading of W. R. Smith's *Kinship and Marriage* led
the writer to question this statement. Professor Moore, in reply,
very reasonably calls attention to early Arabic poetry as his sufficient warrant for the assertion.

animals and leading in all devotional or ritualistic services. Gideon had his private rock or altar upon which he offered sacrifices. Manoah killed a kid and offered it as a burnt-offering to Yahweh. So also Jephthah's vow presupposes on his part priestly functions. Levites are known to have wandered from Judah north and to have taken upon themselves priestly functions which were utilised not alone at sacred places, or sanctuaries, but also privately by individuals as their wealth increased and their burdens multiplied; but before the seventh century they did not crowd aside the heads of families as priests.

The home among these people was a place of gracious and, usually, of abundant hospitality. Not only was it open to him who was discerned to be a man of God, as in the story of Gideon and Manoah, but also to a poor Levite passing through the land. Such a one goes by Jerusalem near nightfall because he questions the hospitality of its alien people, and presses on to Gibeah of Benjamin. The inhospitality of the men of Gibeah the narrator puts over against the generous, even sacred, hospitality of the old man of Ephraim with manifest disapproval. The home shared with the village or with the clan the social features of the religious life. Festivals like those of the vintage and sheep-shearing seem to have been affairs of the village or of the clan; but weddings, in the latter part of the period under consideration, if not earlier, were confined to the home and the family. The bride-groom with his wedding companions went to the house of the bride and took her home, where at his own expense he provided a feast

that often lasted several days and was an occasion of
great good-humour, during which jokes were perpe-
trated and riddles propounded.

There could have been no such extremes of wealth
and poverty among the people as we find in the eighth
century in North Israel. The homes may have been
humble, but actual want was felt only on rare occasions when the Canaanites of the neighbourhood were
jealous and troublesome. Little meat was eaten, but
cereals and fruits, milk and curds, wine and even
stronger drink usually abounded, for the people held
labour in honour and were industrious. Even a man
like Gideon, who could marshal the fighting men of
his own sept or clan and surprise and punish to the
point of utter discomfiture a multitude of Bedouins, was not above threshing wheat for his family
by stealth in a wine-press. The father of a family
was reverenced not only as a well nigh absolute lord,
as is seen in the stories of Achsah and of Jephthah's
daughter, but he was also loved. The family was bound
together by the strongest ties of affection. Polygamy and concubinage were undoubtedly common, but
they probably seldom led to such unpleasantness as
would seem to be indicated by the stories of domestic infelicity found in Genesis, which were coloured
to suit the monogamous ideas of a much later day.
This has its bearing upon the question of child-nurt-
ure in those early times, for, as another has pointed
out, polygamy makes each mother more important to
her own children than the father.[1]

[1] Hastings' *Dictionary*, vol. i., p. 848.

CHAPTER V

PRIMITIVE man seems not to have discriminated sharply between himself and nature. Not only did he think of animals as akin to himself, but he also similarly conceived of inanimate nature. He thought of things about, above, and beyond him as possessed of spirits not unlike his own. Inasmuch as mystery clung to many of these manifestations of life or of energy because they were beyond his knowledge and comprehension, the question of his attitude toward these so-conceived phenomena was to him all-important because to him they were real spiritual existences. Were they propitious or were they evilly inclined? The measure of his success in life was the measure of their favour. If they seemed hostile, he sought to placate them; if propitious, he might easily find ways of rewarding them. Sacrifices were consequently made early, though not by fire. Gifts were exposed in woody dells, or left under great trees; they were cast into wells, rivers, lakes, or seas; they were buried, or, as in the case of drink-offerings, poured out upon the ground. If the gifts exposed were carried off by wild beasts, or, if in other ways they disappeared, they were thought of as accepted; if the gifts cast into the waters were borne away, they were supposed to be accepted. If the offerings were not carried off or borne away, the giver said they had been rejected. There was then naught for him to do but to offer more precious gifts. The drink-offering, if it soaked into the thirsty ground, was well-pleasing to the spirit to whom it had been poured out.

We find traces of the origin of sacrifice among the more primitive customs of Israel during this period, survivals of a life earlier than the nomadic. Indeed, long after this period, wine and blood were poured out. When animals were slaughtered at altars or at thresholds, as they probably were at this time, though efforts to find traces of threshold sacrifices among the early Hebrews seem not to have been successful, the blood was poured out as an offering to God. Though possibly not the earliest form of sacrifice, it must have been a very early form. According to Judges ix. 5, Abimelech appears to have slain his seventy brothers at a sacred stone as an offering to Yahweh that he might escape blood-revenge.[1] Here the blood was poured out. The Book of the Covenant presupposes the offering of the blood. Inasmuch as the Hebrews looked upon the blood of a victim as its life, in their view the life was returned to its source or author by pouring out the blood upon the ground. This custom long survived among the Israelites. We find abundant evidence of it not only in the writings of the Deuteronomists of the seventh century, but also in those of the Priestly School of the fifth and fourth centuries.[2]

[1] Moore, *Judges, I. C.*, p. 242 f.
[2] Deut. xii. 27; Lev. iv. 7, etc.

A beautiful story is told of David that reveals to us why it was that this man who, though not the sweet and inspiring psalmist that we have thought him, could yet inspire confidence and, at least in his younger days and early manhood, win and hold bold, fierce spirits in loyalty to him.[1] In one of his later campaigns against the Philistines he found himself after a hard day in one of his old haunts, the stronghold of Adullam.[2] The wish for a drink of water from the old well by Bethlehem finding audible expression, three of his valiant men slipped out unobserved and made their way at peril of their lives to Bethlehem, got the water for which their leader had longed and returned therewith. David, with the instincts of a high-souled man not insensible of the cost, poured the water out as a drink-offering unto Yahweh. The story has about it the note of reality. The act was characteristic of that rude time which was not utterly wanting in men who could hazard themselves in heroic exploits, as it was not without leaders who could appreciate them.[3] But though the story be a late fabrication, as some appear to regard it, yet it reveals quite as surely a form of sacrifice that must have been common in the days of the Judges.

For the origin of sacrifice among the Hebrews we should not look to the Book of Genesis. The stories of sacrifice found in Genesis contain legendary material worked over by J or E, or by earlier writers,

[1] 2 Sam. xxiii. 15 ff.

[2] A stronghold rather than a cave.—H. P. Smith, *Samuel*, *I. C.*, p. 203.

[3] There is, it is true, the possibility that David looked upon the water thus secured as blood, and feared to drink it.

from a religious motive, thus revealing the conceptions of a later time. Undoubtedly the Priestly Writer was wrong in refusing to speak of sacrifices as happening before the Exodus, when in his thought an Aaronic priesthood was instituted, for sacrifices in accordance with primitive ideas must have been offered by the Hebrews from earliest times.[1] For the earliest trace of sacrifice among the Hebrews we should look to such data as we find in Judges and 1 Samuel, as we shall elsewhere have occasion to note. The victim was slaughtered at some natural rock[2] or on some stone set up for the purpose, not at a regularly constructed altar. Fire had come into use in connection with sacrifice, but, as a rule, only the inwards, the fat, and the head, perhaps, were burnt.[3] In offering these portions, the offerer would not in his own eyes be placing before his God the least valuable parts, for the contrary was the case. The fatty inwards, as the seat of the life, were esteemed peculiarly precious.

But it is upon the social side of sacrifice that we would here especially dwell. Broadly speaking, we may safely say that all sacrifices were feasts of communion and all meals were sacrificial.[4] If the offerer was alone in making his sacrifice, he yet ate with his

[1] Schultz, *American Journal of Theology*, vol. iv., p. 257 ff.

[2] Judges vi. 20; ix. 5; xiii. 19.

[3] It was the fragrance or odour of the burning fat or flesh upon which Yahweh was supposed to feed.—1 Sam. xxvi. 19; Gen. viii. 21; Amos v. 21. This is in accordance with the primitive ideas of all peoples, as Tylor and other anthropologists have shown.

[4] W. Robertson Smith, *The Rel. of the Sem.*, p. 236 f.; H. C. Trumbull, *The Cov. of Salt.*

God in a common meal; if not alone, then all who participated in the sacrifice shared also in the common meal, the feasting being one of the most conspicuous features of the sacrifice. We have alluded before to the father of the family as the priest of the household. It was not until the Book of Deuteronomy was written in the seventh century that an effort was made, which could have been but partially successful, to restrict sacrifice to one central sanctuary and to confine the priestly function to one clan, the Levites, who had from the time of the Judges grown in favour as priests. Heads of families, elders of clans, and men like Saul and David and Solomon, the rulers of Israel, performed, with great acceptance to the people, priestly functions.

Probably, in early Israel the head of a single household or family did not make an offering of an ox or sheep as often as leading men made communal offerings in clans and villages,[1] towns and cities. Such slaughter would be an occasion of some importance to a people that did not make large use of flesh as food. Connected with these feasts would be certain religious rites with sacrifices of portions. The men of a sept or clan or village would come together to kill a lamb or a bullock. As a sacred custom not to be ignored, the blood of the victim would be poured out to Yahweh, or to the local Baal, and the inwards burnt as the portion of the God worshipped. But, if

---

[1] Such offerings were, of course, communal. The altar was a place of slaughter. W. Robertson Smith, p. 322, *The Rel. of the Sem.* It was also, as the high place, a place of feasting. Budde, *The Rel. of Is. to the Ex.*, p. 23.

the occasion was not one of peculiar danger or so-
lemnity, the feast would be the chief feature of the
occasion. This seems to be the thought of W. R.
Smith. "Long before any public revenue was set apart
for the maintenance of sacrificial ritual, the ordinary
type of Hebrew worship was essentially social, for in
antiquity all religion was the affair of the community
rather than of the individual. A sacrifice was a public ceremony of a township or of a clan, and private
householders were accustomed to reserve their offerings for the annual feasts, satisfying their religious
feelings in the interval by vows to be discharged
when the festal season came round. Then the crowds
streamed into the sanctuary from all sides, dressed in
their gayest attire, marching joyfully to the sound of
music, and bearing with them not only the victims
appointed for sacrifice but store of bread and wine to
set forth the feast. The law of the feast was open-
handed hospitality; no sacrifice was complete without guests, and portions were freely distributed to
rich and poor within the circle of a man's acquaint-
ance. Universal hilarity prevailed, men ate and drank
and were merry together, rejoicing before their God." [1]

Late as the story may be, the account of such a
feast in 1 Samuel ix. must reflect the characteristics
of the early Hebrew sacrificial feast. Here we see the
elders of the village assembled on occasion at a high
place, the usual place for such an assembly.[2] They
are expecting to entertain Samuel, who appears

[1] *Rel. of the Sem.*, p. 236 f.
[2] H. P. Smith, *Samuel, I. C.*, p. 59 ff. ; Schultz, *Old Test.
Theo.*, vol. i., p. 65, in speaking of E, remarks : " The holy places

at such times, not as a theocratic ruler or as a
high-priest, but as a man of God, or head of the
Shiloh sanctuary. He is to be their guest of honour,
to give, as such, peculiar dignity, if not peculiar sanctity, to the occasion. He is not necessary to such a
gathering, but the occasion means more if he is with
them. In this feast, as in all feasts in which animals
were eaten as food, Yahweh shared, but it was the
feast that was the central idea or feature of the assembly in their eyes. The modern picnic, though seldom
of such an exclusive character, is undoubtedly a survival of such primitive gatherings, just as the New
England donation-party is a survival of a later custom, that of sending a portion of a victim slain to the
legally constituted priest. On this occasion there was
some delay, as Samuel lingered for Saul, whom he
took with him to the company assembling in the hall
of feasting, or common dining-room connected with
the high place. Thirty of the elders or free citizens
of the village thus came together. Samuel and Saul
were welcomed. The choicest piece of meat was placed
before Saul at Samuel's suggestion. It is not difficult
for us to picture to our minds such a gathering, in
which flesh and wine were partaken of generously,
and good cheer abounded. These occasions were
undoubtedly frequent.[1] By bringing together the

of Israel, against the worship at which Amos and Hosea are already
fighting with passionate zeal, are, to this historian objects of perfectly unembarrassed joy and admiration."

[1] 1 Sam. xx. 6, 29 ; cf. 1 Sam. i. 3 ; ii. 19. It is extremely
probable that in the early time such feasts were held at the new
moon ; cf. 2 Kings iv. 23 ; 1 Chron. xxiii. 31; Amos viii. 5;
Hosea ii. 11 ; Isaiah i. 13, 14.

freemen of a village or city more informally than
when they came to discuss matters of public policy
in a legally constituted assembly, they made possible talk upon matters of common concern, as they
also furnished occasion for the interchange of thought
and feeling in other directions. It is no wonder that
the worship of the high places should have survived
until long after Josiah's day, and that the people
should have looked with disfavour upon the Deuteronomist in his attempt to abolish them. As the
common places of slaughter and of feasting, the high
places might easily permit of various forms of excess ;
in the early time they must have partaken largely of
the character of the gross Baal worship, in whose honour the Israelites came together. All was rough and
hearty, not unlike the old manorial feasts of feudal
days in Britain and upon the Continent, with talk,
strong and pure at times, or coarse wit and repartee
at other times, enlivened now and then with folk-
story and song. Yet, perhaps, just because these
feasts were of this character, they must have played a
conspicuous and not altogether unwholesome part
in the development of the social life of the people.
They belonged to an early stage of culture. As the
people became more civilised, they outgrew them ; it
was probably quite as much because they had grown
away from them as because of their character that
they were finally abolished.

CHAPTER VI

THE INFLUENCE OF INDIVIDUALS

IT is a mistake to suppose that in a state of society like that in Israel in the days of the Judges, which to us must seem crude and unorganised, the individual, though possessed of strong qualities or unusual talents of some kind, had no opportunities for their exercise, for the fact is, such an environment creates or produces just the men it needs for peculiar and difficult tasks, or for what may prove to them delightful services.[1] Opportunities may, it is true, be limited, the theatre for the exercise of unusual gifts may be small, but the capacity for something outside the ordinary has not to cease for want of exercise. Considering the time covered by the period of the Judges, some two and a half or three centuries, which carry us to the close of the life of Saul (for his life, as does the life of Samuel, falls within this period) we have but few stories of remarkable men, few names, indeed, of such—fewer than we have been wont to think, if the names of the so-called minor Judges are simply clan names, as has been lately surmised. Many men may have come into some sort of local prominence, distin-

---

[1] Budde, *Rel. of Is. to Ex.*, pp. 78, 79 ; Moore, *Judges, P.*, pp. 44, 55 ; Hastings' *Dictionary*, vol. ii., p. 815 ; Driver, *Intro. to L. of O. T.*, p. 157 ff., 1st ed.; p. 167 ff., 8th ed.

guishing themselves in battle or in other ways, for
society was far from being organised solely on a war
basis, but few such are mentioned in the fragmentary
literary remains of the period. And the leading men
celebrated in folk-story or song, as Gideon or Jephthah, for example, probably played a much smaller part
territorially and in point of time than is commonly
supposed. Only in the thought of later time, in the
days of the kings, were they regarded as judges or
rulers who exercised authority for long periods over
all Israel. They could at the most have done little
more than incite their own and neighbouring clans
at a time of some great peril, and so vindicate those
interested and involved. In doing this they made
a name for themselves, so that the people thought
of them as available in case they should again find
themselves in extremity. In rare instances, as apparently was the case with Abimelech, they might
be inclined to usurp authority and might be able to
lord it over their fellow-clansmen, but as a rule they
became little more than inspirational centres around
which thought and grateful affection crystallised;
their influence was moral rather than physical.
Where their achievements were so noteworthy as
to pass into folk-story or song, their influence must
have been incalculably felt by their contempora-
ries and by later generations. In some instances
they may have become the permanent leaders or
chiefs of their clans during life, but as a rule the
civil heads were men who had less remarkably distinguished themselves. We know almost nothing
of the civil heads of clans. Then, as now, the man

who did the unusual thing was the man who was
honoured. The laborious civil servants, very likely,
received as their reward, abundant contemporary
criticism, and at their demise speedy oblivion. Of
such men there must have been many in Israel.
These more obscure men were potent influences in
shaping and in giving character to the clans, though
they may have done little as compared with the military leaders and heroes in the way of unifying these
clans. Unfortunately, we know next to nothing of
these men, and it is unreasonable to suppose that
later investigations will greatly aid us here. In
speaking, then, of the influence of individuals upon
the social life of the period, we must necessarily dwell
chiefly upon those leaders of whose lives we have
fragmentary stories which contain at least a few authentic, indisputable facts and a considerable body
of sociological data. That there were many more
who were worthy of mention, and who for a time were
celebrated in song, is undoubtedly true. Scholars are
not amiss in discovering reasons for the retention of
most of the hero-tales that have been preserved. The
more perplexing question which they have to face,
and cannot answer, has to do with the number and
achievements of those whose names even have disappeared.

We begin with Samson, for of Joshua little of a reliable nature is known. Very likely Joshua was the
leader who saw the principal clans across the Jordan ;
he may also, as the ablest man of the tribe of Joseph,
have had much to do with securing the highlands of
Central Canaan, though probably not as much there,

and certainly not as much elsewhere, as late tradition accredits him with having. He was, let us believe, a wiser, humaner man than we have been wont
to think him, a fearless soldier, and, at the same time,
it may be, a sort of civil magistrate. Much of this is
mere supposition, for, so far as we know, Joshua found
small place in the literature of his age ; but it probably has the advantage of according with facts more
closely than do the stories of the barbarities practised by him in the settlement of Canaan.

The story of Samson as it has come down to us is
late, belonging to a time not long prior to the days of
Samuel.[1] The Philistines are in the ascendant and
are already harassing Dan and Judah, as they were
later to trouble all Central and Southern Canaan.
But the original of this folk-tale must be very old,
belonging undoubtedly to the earliest period, and it
must, if we are to get at its social significance, be so
studied. About it there is more of the fabulous, the
marvellous, than about the other stories. The parents
are visited by the Messenger of Yahweh, and not only
given an intimation of the conception and birth of
the child, but also instructions as to how the mother
shall live during pregnancy and how she shall rear
her son when born. With the ascending flame of the
sacrifice offered by Manoah, the messenger goes up
into heaven. The story then passes on to the young

[1] Kittel, *His. of Heb.*, vol. ii., p. 91, declares, " The story moves
uncertainly amid myth and legend and history. It belongs to none
of them wholly ; each claims a share in it." Yet Dr. Kittel thinks
that much of it is capable of a satisfactory historical explanation.
With this conclusion we must agree. Efforts to discover mythical
elements in the story have not been remarkably successful.

manhood of Samson, with the intimation that the boy grew, that Yahweh blessed him, and that the spirit of Yahweh began to stir him.

Then comes the narrative of his nearly consummated marriage with a woman of Timnath, a few miles southwest of Zorah in Dan, his birthplace and home, in which narrative his first labour or exploit (Samson is the Hebrew Heracles, and his exploits are not unlike the labours of the Greek Heracles) is related. On his way to visit the Timnath maiden, he comes alone upon a fierce lion, and feeling the demonic fury seize him, he catches and slays the beast, rending him with his hands, as one might rend a kid.[1] Returning, not long after, he finds the carcass of the lion contains honey, the rapidity with which all this has come about being part of the marvel of the story. This leads to a riddle, a poor one by the way, on the part of Samson during the festivities of the wedding. The solving of the riddle, which was to be amply rewarded, was made possible through the worming of the story out of Samson, on the last day of the feast, by the bride, who had been threatened in a way characteristic of those rough times by the wedding companions, who spoke of burning home and bride and family. They were apparently equal to such conduct, as the sequel of the story reveals. That there were men in those days, even in Hebrew communities, vile, worthless, lawless men, who were capable of even worse crimes than this, we know from the story of the outrage of Gibeah and other folk-tales of the time. Indignant over the

[1] See Appendix VI.

treachery practised at his wedding, Samson went home, leaving his discomfited bride to be given in marriage to one of his companions. Later, in time of harvest, Samson went down to Timnath, as though his marriage had been consummated, expecting to visit this woman as his wife, taking the usual morning gift, a kid.[1] The father intercepted him. Incensed, Samson went out and wrought vengeance upon the Canaanites, performing what to us must seem the most incredible of all his labours, the destruction of the standing grain of his enemies with foxes tied together, tail to tail, with fire-brands between, after having been caught for this purpose, no small feat.[2] Vengeance having been wrought upon the unoffending woman and her family, Samson is again aroused. A multitude of Canaanites, how we are not told, are slain ; and then, as though for once fearful, Samson takes refuge in the Shephelah of Judah. Followed, he is sought by the men of Judah, who, with his consent, bind him and deliver him into the hands of his old foes. Again the demonic power comes upon the man, and freeing himself easily, with the green jaw-bone of an ass he kills a thousand men, another marvellous labour, and does thereafter what seems to us as wonderful coming from him

[1] Gen. xxxviii. 20.

[2] Hastings' *Dictionary*, vol. ii., p. 64, G. E. Post, article, *Fox*, admits that שׁוּעָל is used of both the jackal and the fox, but the writer referring to this incident remarks : " This would be well nigh impossible in the case of foxes, which are shy, solitary animals, but not difficult in that of jackals, which are gregarious." This scholar fails to perceive that the marvellous preponderates in this folk-story ; in it impossibilities vanish; nothing is incredible.

—turns his exploit into poetry. A story of miracle follows. This man of many devices and of gigantic resources being athirst and in extremity in a dry land, has a rock cleft for him, out of which water flows to revive his spirits. Next we find him off across the plain in Gaza, not far from the Egyptian frontier. The men of Gaza either watch without the city-wall or sleep with eye open, in the thought that they must take their renowned and unsavoury guest betimes in the morning; but Samson rises at midnight and goes forth, carrying upon his shoulders the mighty gates of the city, bearing them off and up to Hebron, a little jaunt in the night of over thirty miles.

The next move on the part of Samson is in the way of a love-affair. He goes down into the vale of Sorek and falls in love with and pays court to a harlot, being peculiarly susceptible to female charms. Through her the Canaanites seek to reach her lover and to shear him of his strength. Various experiments are made; but it is not until he is importuned with tears that Samson yields. Then, with head resting in his mistress' lap he is shorn of his great locks and therewith of his gigantic strength. The old demonic fury comes not upon him as the familiar cry is heard and he goes forth to shake himself. Helpless, he is seized and blinded, and being cast into a prison-house, is made, as his contribution to the labour of the prison, to turn the mill in which the corn is daily ground. But one more important episode is in store for him, one more labour is to be performed before he passes off the stage.

A feast in honour of their god, a local deity, is made at Gaza whither Samson has been taken. The blind man is brought in to be mocked and to furnish sport for the multitude; but upon them come confusion and death as the mighty hero, in the one great and only sublime exploit of his life, bows himself and presses out the great pillars upon which the roof rests, and so brings the building down, crushing himself and the people in the overthrow. It may be surmised that the original story contained the records of actual deeds wrought by one or more of Israel's strong men, and as such had its local influence in the west and south; but in its present form it must have amused, fascinated, and stirred many a member of the clan of Dan, and of other clans as well. Mixed in character though its influence must have been morally, it still must, on the whole, have incited to faith in Yahweh, the wonder-worker, and must have led to heroic and, let us hope, to more disinterested exploits. The element of the marvellous may have rendered it the more interesting; but it may be that a vein of humour running through the story was recognised and that this rendered it not unwholesome in its influence; that it may in truth have kept it from inciting to what in practice a pure ethics must condemn, for the Hebrews were not without this sense of humour and were none the worse for having it.

Among the northern clans the one person to stand forth conspicuously in the early time, so far as we are able to judge, was Deborah, though Barak appears not far behind as a worthy second. The overthrow of Jabin of Hazor by the clans of Issachar and Naphtali seems to have antedated the overthrow of Sisera and the Canaanite confederacy. The stories should not be confounded as different versions of the same campaign, but the second story, and that only as it comes out in the Song of Deborah, can be implicitly depended upon. Here a woman of Issachar with a colleague, Barak of Naphtali, incites her own and certain other clans and overthrows the Canaanites.[1] The character of Deborah as it is suggested must have been such as to have stirred Israel to patriotic fervour and heroic exploit. There was nothing in the story of Jael to offend their sentiments as a people to whom the duty of hospitality was sacred. Sisera appears at the tent-door asking for drink as he flees, and as he puts his head into the bowl to drink the milk or curds she hands him, she, with no little peril to herself, smites him with the tent-mallet a staggering blow upon the forehead, thus felling him to the ground.[2] In the curse pronounced upon the faithless inhabitants of Meroz for failing to do their part, and in the sarcastic taunts thrown at the recreant clans of Dan and Asher and Reuben, we see a moral influence, coming directly, to be sure, from the personality of the unknown author of the ode, yet regarded by the Hebrews of a later day as emanating from Deborah, who really inspired it as well as made it possible.

Ehud, the saviour from the Moabites, and it may

[1] Judges v. ; Cheyne and Black, *Encyc. Bib.*, vol. i., c. 1047 f. ; Hastings' *Dictionary*, vol. ii., p. 807 f. ; Moore, *Judges, I. C.*, pp. 107–173 ; Budde, *Folk-Songs of Is.*, *The New World*, March, 1893.

[2] Moore, *Judges, P.*, p. 66.

be from the Ammonites, stands forth as a man of his time, crafty, grim, and bloody. He did his work relentlessly, and, supplemented as he was by Ephraim at the ford of the Jordan, freed his people from a real peril, for there was danger that these kindred clans would follow after and crowd out, or what might have been as unfortunate, absorb the Hebrews. We cannot forbear the thought that Ehud's deed was secretly regarded with detestation and that his influence upon later ages was unimportant.

The danger from which Gideon saved Israel, the frequent if not the permanent devastation of their fields in the north and east by the Midianites or Bedouins, was also a real danger. The story is not free from the marvellous as we have it. This son of Joash is beating out wheat stealthily when the Messenger of Yahweh greets him as a man of valour, inciting him to undertake the task of ridding his region of these hosts, and assuring him that Yahweh is with him. This he doubts, as he does his own ability, and he pleads his unimportance. Urged further, he asks that he may be permitted to refresh his guest, whom he takes to be simply a man of God. The viands prepared are not used as food but are consumed upon the rock or altar by fire as the staff of the Messenger of Yahweh touches them. With further words of assurance, Gideon is left. Later, demonic fury comes upon him, and he, taking three hundred of his clansmen, makes his way to the camp of the Midianites. With his page or armour-bearer he visits the camp of the enemy by night and overhears the men as they talk, and so discovers their timorous, panicky state.

This susceptibility to confusion is taken advantage of. Supplying his men with earthen jars and torches, he surprises the camp, throws all into confusion and routs them, and so wins the day. The fugitives are pursued and overtaken with slaughter, and their two kings being made captive, are afterward slain. The sequel is characteristic of the times. An ephod-idol is made of the spoil of gold and is set up by Gideon as an object of divination and worship, apparently with no thought of incurring disfavour. Gideon as a leader among his own clansmen must have exercised after this considerable influence; and later in its simplest form his story must have had a happy effect upon the members of other clans as well as his own. Not so Abimelech, his Shechemite son. This man was not without resources of a kind; certainly Gaal ben Obed as an adventurer was no match for him, though he carried all before him when he entered Shechem with his kinsmen freebooters. But he was too selfish a man to be of any real use to his clan. Fortunately, his career was cut short.

Jephthah, though impetuous, thoughtless, and rash, stands forth more clearly and more inspiringly. Even had he possessed the insight to see that he might innocently retract his rash vow, and by substitution of a kid or ram, as in the Abraham story, which, however, could hardly have been known to him,[1] have

[1] Not known, because as a story (Gen. xxii.) it belonged to a later day, and because it had little, if any, basis in fact, save that men in the time of the composition of E were beginning to look with disfavour upon human sacrifices. Even Saul, after Jonathan had become taboo, escaped from his dilemma only by the insistence of the people, who provided a substitute, apparently a human being.

spared his daughter, he could not in so doing have kept his influence. To the men of his day a vow was well nigh as irrevocable as death. But the beauty of this folk-tale, and its power, grew largely out of the heroism, the filial devotion, and piety of this dis- interested maiden of Gilead. Like the name of Deborah, hers shines undimmed to-day, despite the crude and superstitious ideas which enveloped and held her. Had the Hebrews of their day preserved for us from this period naught save the stories of these two women in the way of literary material, we should still be immeasurably their debtors. And if our hearts thrill as we read of these women, how must it have been with devout Hebrews then and since? These were the greater lights that among the mothers and daughters of the various Hebrew clans, even the rudest, were uncertainly and somewhat fearfully try- ing to leave behind a meagre, wandering, for a richer, settled life. There were many of lesser brilliancy as worthy in every way as they, who, within the home and without it, were doing their part to subdue and mould the more ungovernable spirits and passions of their husbands and brothers.

To one who has not studied this period critically it may at first seem strange to find the name of Saul enrolled among the so-called Judges, as are Gideon and Jephthah, instead of classing him with the kings, and studying the story of his life as revealing data that have to do with the social life of the people under the monarchy. But that it must be so studied is now evi- dent. We have seen that the Judges were not, in the proper sense of the term, judges, that they rather were vindicators of their clans, or, at most, of a few clans besides their own, in some great emergency. Saul was little more than this. He did unquestionably serve the people of a larger area, and for a longer period, largely because of the peril to which they were exposed through the coming of the warlike Philistines into prominence. We may even admit that the story of Saul in its simplest form reveals the beginnings of a veritable kingdom or monarchy; yet we must recognise that while the time of Saul marked a transition to another form of civil and social life, there was about it more that was characteristic of the earlier than of the later period.

There are sections of 1 Samuel in which Saul figures prominently that bear unmistakable marks of having been very largely manufactured, or composed, by late writers or editors, that are worth little to the student of Samuel's life, and as little to those who wish to become informed as to the life of Saul. Passages which represent Samuel as a judge and theocratic guide or ruler, and reveal on his part a jealousy of Saul's early popularity that culminated in certain attempts to discredit him in the eyes of the people, must be viewed suspiciously. Saul was as much a man of his time as Gideon was of his. Though his life ended in darkness and gloom, he wrought mightily as a bulwark against the rising tide of Philistinism, yet, for the most part hopelessly, for he did not succeed in crushing Israel's enemies. If only his life had closed earlier, his name might appear as one of the most inspiring in the early annals of the Hebrews.

This is the simple story. The asses of Kish, a man of Benjamin, having wandered away, his son Saul, a stalwart man, was sent with a servant in search of them. After wandering for a considerable time about among the hills of Ephraim in their bootless quest, Saul, discouraged, proposed to return, when, at the suggestion of his servant, he turned aside to a certain city where was Samuel, the seer, who was supposed by divination to help a man in such extremity. Petty work for a man of God it must seem to us, but it was not so considered then. As Saul had not the where-withal to fee the seer, the servant, in his eagerness, produced his bit of silver that would serve the pur-pose. Guided, they made their way to the neighbour-ing high place, where were gathered the elders, or free-holders, of the village for a sacrificial feast, at which the visiting seer was to be their honoured guest. Here Saul was welcomed and shown distinction. Having been entertained by Samuel over night, he was waked by his host in the early morning that he might speed him on his way. Without the city gate, unobserved, Samuel anointed as his choice the modest and won-dering man, thus consecrating him to Yahweh as the ruler of his people, the leader of his hosts in battle, as one eminently fit for a deliverer from the Philistine yoke.[1] Had private converse with him revealed the young man's temper and his strong feeling over his people's peril and distress, such feeling as was sure to ally him later with the ardent patriots known as sons of the prophets—a guild that Samuel apparently largely influenced, if indeed he was not the founder

[1] A different story is told in 1 Sam. x. 17–27.

of it? It is more than probable. We are told that later when Saul met a band of these young men coming down from a high place with music and patriotic ode, he who had been anointed and incited by Samuel, joined them as one of them in spirit and purpose. Stirred mightily by demonic fury, as Gideon and other of the early vindicators of Israel had been, Saul was immediately recognised by the people as one of the leaders among these patriots. Opportunity came soon after for Saul to vindicate Israel. The Ammonites invested Jabesh-Gilead. So sore pressed were the people, that by stealth they sent men across the Jordan for succour. The messengers reached Gibeah of Benjamin, the city of Saul, at an opportune time. Stirred by their story, demonic fury came upon the man. Cutting in pieces in their furrow the steers with which he had been ploughing, Saul sent throughout Benjamin and Ephraim the pieces with the announcement: "Whosoever cometh not forth after Saul and Samuel, so shall it be done unto his steers." Thus aroused, the men of Ephraim and Benjamin rallied, and Jabesh-Gilead was freed from the Ammonite terror. All this was apparently in line with Samuel's wish; there was no sign of disfavour as there was not as manifestly any reluctance on his part when, later, the people themselves came to Samuel to make known their wish that this valiant man of the clan of Benjamin be their accredited leader, saying, "Who is he that said, Saul shall not reign over us? bring the men, that we may put them to death." Thus was Saul publicly chosen as leader or vindicator. That Judah never really had much to do in the way of supporting

Saul seems evident; that many of the northern clans never rallied about him and his house appears evident also. His own clansmen and a few nearby men of Ephraim appear to have made choice of him and to have stood by him to the last, because he seemed their most available man. He who had humbled Ammon was, in their thought, the man to humble the haughty Philistines.

Some two years later, at Micmash, the next great opportunity came to Saul. He blew the horn and straightway there gathered together a few hundred men from the neighbouring country. In the meantime his son Jonathan, by falling upon the Philistine garrison at Geba, had given the signal of the revolt from the hated oppressors on the part of Israel. But so small was the company of men under Saul that the Philistines, unapprehensive of serious trouble, divided themselves into companies for foraging purposes. This gave Israel their watched-for advantage. Jonathan again was the first to act. With an armour-bearer he climbed a hill and stampeded a company of Philistines encamped in the neighbourhood. Saul and his men joined in the pursuit, and the enemy suffered great slaughter, leaving behind at the same time vast spoil. Saul, for reasons of his own, laid a taboo upon all food, so that his men grew faint ere the day closed, and did not make as much of a success of the rout of the Philistines as otherwise they might have done. Jonathan, not knowing of the taboo, ate some wild honey which he happened upon, thus becoming, according to the ideas of those times, himself taboo. But for the intercession of the people and their provision of a substitute, probably a human being, he would have been put to death. When at last the people did eat flesh it was that which was unclean of its blood, because it was raw or because it had been killed apart from any altar, and was unconsecrated. When Saul discovered this he had an altar hastily constructed, and ordered that all sheep and oxen should be slaughtered according to custom at the altar thus built. There can be little doubt that after this Saul kept the enemies of Israel considerably in check.

In process of time Saul's mind revealed signs of insanity or melancholia; and David ben Jesse, a man of war and affairs, and withal a skilful harpist, was brought to the court as a member of Saul's body-guard, or one of his armour-bearers, in the thought that he might be of service to the King. Perhaps it was not until after he had joined the company that stood near Saul that his skill as a harpist was noted and it occurred to anyone to make special use of him in restoring Saul from time to time to his right mind. However this may be, we know he was thus used with most happy results; but that later, after David had in some way revealed his ability as a valorous man of war, and the women at the entering in of the gate had lauded him above Saul as the hero of the hour, Saul became jealous of him, looking upon him as a possible rival. So did his jealousy increase that he was moved to put David farther from his presence. Attempts were made by imperilling him to get rid of him altogether; but all efforts failed, and the man grew in favour in the eyes of the people.

An attempt having been made upon his life, David fled from the neighbourhood, and for years lived the life of an outlaw, showing in some instances, as most outlaws have ever been wont to do, respect for the rights of property of some men, but living for the most part upon the forced gratuities levied upon various individuals and clans, and upon the booty secured from hostile tribes. We need not trace the rapidly declining sun of Saul's life as it darkened more and more toward its close. Enough to note that Saul's earlier life, properly studied, presents no such blemishes as the late editors of the old folk-lore and traditions seemed to discover. Until the malady, which was a misfortune rather than a personally reprehensible fault, he was a vindicator among the vindicators of Israel. His jealousy of David was mean and petty, and undid in its resultant consequences the good that he wrought in the earlier years of his public career, and left such an impression upon the memory of men as rendered it easy for late redactors of the history of the time to use him as a dark background upon which to picture the monarchy that was to endure in Judah for four centuries.

The growing prominence of certain of the great sanctuaries, and of those who officiated at them, is seen in the story of Eli, who lived in the days of the earlier Philistine domination. Probably, as the Israelites found themselves imperilled, they may have looked more and more to Yahweh and his Ark, the symbol of his presence and his might. Certainly the loss of it meant the downfall of Eli and his house. Samuel,

the real successor and inheritor of the best for which
Eli had stood, became a more prominent factor in the
life of the people through his encouragement of that
new and strange movement that furnished an outlet
for ardent patriotism known as the prophetic guild
or school of the prophets.   The story of his life
was so worked over by late redactors, who made of
him a theocratic ruler, a second Moses, that it is
difficult, if not impossible, for us to make the keeper
of the Shiloh sanctuary stand forth in such a way as
to determine his influence.   His great work was undoubtedly that in which the prophetic guild so admirably supplemented him, the revival of a sense of
unity, or the partial creation thereof, among these
Hebrew clans.   Just here, Saul, as his choice, proved
for long a great helper, as David, his later and hap-
pier choice, did afterward as a leader and ruler. Still,
so long as Saul remained himself, Samuel seems to
have stood at his side to encourage him ; it was
probably not until Saul's mind began to give way that
Samuel turned, as the people themselves showed a
disposition to do, to David.   As we shall have occasion in another place to speak of the growing nationalism at length, more need not be said at this point, for
we are now interested in the great men of Israel as
forces in the social, rather than the civic, life. Upon
David we need not dwell, for his real influence belongs to the period of the monarchy.

   A word as to the social significance of all this.   It
is a noteworthy fact that these records tell of no
wrong of a purely personal character that was avenged,
nor of any purely personal exploit.   The wrongs were

regarded as social rather than individual ; they were looked upon as offences against a clan or against the Hebrew people. So, too, the exploits narrated were thought of as performed or achieved for the clan of which the doer was a member, or for his own and neighbouring clans. The story of the outrage at Gibeah may perplex us, for we may not be able to understand it, but it is safe to say that if it happened as told, the outrage was felt to be an offence against the inviolable rights of hospitality, if not against the common sentiments of humanity. The labours of Samson may seem to us like deeds of a purely personal character, in which a man of great strength got a little needed exercise, and at the same time revenged himself upon his personal enemies. Probably, they were not so regarded by the Hebrews. These old stories have for us a new meaning when we grasp their social significance. So to conceive of them is to lift them as literature up into the higher regions in which moral ideals are seen to have some place, though those ideals were in many respects vastly inferior to those of Jesus Christ. The individual who came into social and civic, and, it may be, military prominence among these early Israelites, had, it should be noticed, relatively more influence toward the close of the period than earlier ; but this is what we should naturally expect, not alone because of the peculiar peril which threatened Israel, but also because society had become more developed. The greater the extent to which social integration is carried, the larger the opportunity for the individual of exceptional talent. In character the folk-lore tales of 1 Samuel are scarcely, if at all, superior to those of the Judges. It is only when they are closely scrutinised that the fact that they reveal a somewhat advanced social state appears. So, too, as regards the place of certain prominent men. Without careful critical study the place of individuals cannot be determined nor their influence upon the social life of the people be estimated with any degree of exactitude.

CHAPTER VII

INDUSTRY, TRADE, AND TRAVEL

AMONG the members of a clan there was, we may safely assume, considerable social intercourse. The limited extent of territory occupied by a clan would render this easily possible, even though highways were few and poor, and the importance of the clan as an organisation would necessitate this. Each family may have been largely dependent upon its own resources; each city most certainly was so dependent. Still, on questions of public policy, in the settlement of individual controversies that were beyond the jurisdiction or power of the elders who sat in the gates, in the arrangement of marriages, etc., there must have been occasion for frequent communication between the different parts of a clan. While wagons were used but little, save for local purposes, being too cumbrous, saddled asses were common, and they furnished a convenient and fairly comfortable means of locomotion between neighbouring and even distant cities. "A comparison of the passages in which חֲמוֹר (he-ass) and אָתוֹן (she-ass) respectively occur," as an Old Testament student has remarked, "shows that the former was more used for carrying burdens and for agriculture, the latter for riding. Hence some have thought that אָתוֹן denotes a superior breed and not simply she-ass; but this opinion is now given up. We must conclude that she-asses were preferred for riding. As the name shows, the Eastern ass is generally reddish in colour; white asses are rarer, and, therefore, used by the rich and distinguished."[1]

The home-life of the people was far from being a life of isolation and absolute privacy, for the home was usually in village or city, in a centre that pulsated placidly, after the Eastern fashion, rather than violently, with life and activity. Where agriculture is carried on according to primitive methods, a moderately fertile district permits of a considerable population. It is only when, as in our own day, farming is done by machinery that agriculturalists lead a lonely life; where work is done by hand, many hands are needed. Men must perforce be brought together and must toil side by side, and at certain seasons women must bear their part, if custom will allow it, so giving to the social side of labour an element of colour. The Hebrew clans may have been slow in adjusting themselves to the new environment, and may have depended for a long time largely upon their flocks and herds, but, even so, they were not isolated because their life was of necessity, under the circumstances, a village life. The young man might lead forth the flock to pasture in the morning for a day of quiet vigils, but he came back at night with his charge to fold it within or near the village. Life was probably not as insecure during ordinary times as we have thought. Rough men might betake themselves to a life of outlawry, as

[1] Cheyne and Black, *Encyc. Bib.*, vol. i., c. 344.

did Gaal ben Obed and Jephthah and David, but they may have depended largely upon the plunder of caravans, and even here may, as a rule, have levied toll or tribute, or something that seemed akin to it, instead of making entire spoil thereof, as was the case in actual warfare. The unfortunate state of things in the north in the days of Deborah, when caravans ceased and the few who travelled betook themselves to by-paths, is spoken of as though it were exceptional, as it probably was. Ordinarily nothing is said of the difficulty of communication, and the passing of men and women from place to place is not referred to as extraordinary. If the so-called Blessing of Jacob, late as it is, may be used as illustrative of those times, there are certain passages not to be overlooked, for they bear upon the social life of their day with great force. Take the allusion to Benjamin, a clan in a narrow and infertile region northeast of Jerusalem :

> Benjamin is a wolf that raveneth :
> In the morning he shall devour the prey,
> And in the evening he shall divide the spoil.[1]

So, too, take the passage referring to Dan, a clan that had at the time gone up into the East Lebanon region under the shadows of Hermon, and was therefore favourably situated for the spoiling of caravans :

> Dan shall be a serpent in the way,
> An adder in the path,
> That biteth at the horse's heels
> So that the rider falleth backward.[2]

[1] Gen. xlix. 27.   [2] Gen. xlix. 17.

Akin to these are the words concerning Judah that had territory more advantageously located as a rendezvous for freebooters than for agriculture.

The location of Canaan was favourable for trade. Highways were few, but in a land where the soil is such as for the most part is found there, paths could easily be worn and could be kept by constant travel in a fairly passable state. Travellers, it is true, could find no inns along the way ; they must carry food for themselves and for their asses ; still, inasmuch as the home was a place of gracious and generous hospitality, such travellers could seldom have suffered neglect. Though a night in the open country under the wondrous Eastern sky was not to be dreaded, it is unlikely that passengers had often to tarry without village or city gate. The pictures of the hospitable entertainment of guests which we find in the literature of the period under consideration are such as stir us to-day when a gently nurtured Christian woman may, while utilising modern conveniences, pass from place to place, from city to city, and encounter naught but a bald officialism which may refuse even the barest courtesies of life unless tips are freely dispensed. The charm of it does not belong wholly, by any means, we should remind ourselves, to the literary material in which it is depicted, but to the real life of the people which is set forth with fidelity to local colour and conditions.

That the Hebrews learned many of the arts of life of the Canaanites after they settled among them, we have already remarked.[1] The original sources of the

[1] Piepenbring, *His. du Peuple d'Is.*, pp. 96–100.

period mention manufactures of various kinds which have to do, not alone with a nomadic and an agricultural stage, but also with a social state considerably advanced. Mention is made of bowstrings and war-horns, of shields and spears, of shepherd's pipes and ox-goads, of doors and locks, of chairs and tables, of razors or shears, of cords and ropes, of dyed stuffs and embroidery, of the vine and barley, of wine and strong drink. But one conclusion is possible; it is that the Israelites were quick to learn of their neighbours, and that they were for the most part on such friendly terms with them that the civilisation of the one people easily became, with slight modifications, the civilisation of the other people. This is the thought of another. " Living close together, and often enough associating in a peaceable way with the former possessors of the land, could not fail to exert its influence also on Israel's moral and intellectual life. Israel entered on the inheritance of a much richer and more advanced civilisation than that which it had itself as yet commanded. The industrial art and discoveries of Phœnicia, still more perhaps the art and civilisation of the Euphrates and Egypt that Phœnicia had borrowed, were, through the active trade relations subsisting, soon the property of Israel. Its horizon was widened; knowledge and interests, but with them also needs and enjoyments, that had up to this time remained unknown to this rough desert people, were made accessible to them." [1]

Eastern cities had their squares, or open spaces within their gates, in which friends might meet each

[1] Kittel, *His. of the Heb.*, vol. ii., p. 94 f.

other, where strangers might tarry until someone felt
moved to offer them hospitality, and where trade might
be prosecuted, the open space serving frequently as
a market-place. Here, too, or outside the gate, the
people came together whenever matters of common
concern impelled them, and it apparently took little
to bring out the whole population of a village or of
a city. A fresh bit of intelligence from beyond their
walls, a vague rumour of impending disaster, the coming of some well-known personage, this, and even less,
might empty all homes of both old and young. Between cities of the same clan there may have been
little occasion for trade, but the passing of caravans
from place to place linked such cities together and so
helped to keep them in touch with each other. On
the whole, then, we may speak of the time as one in
which life was not socially isolated. If there was
such communication and intercourse as made possible
the propagation and dissemination of evil, there was
through this same social interchange opportunity for
good influences to pass from village to village, and
from city to city. The mind could not have stagnated.
Life was alert and active. If competition was not
keen, intercourse was unrestricted and frequent. The
social instincts of the people may not have been of the
purest, but they found satisfaction; and it was probably better so. The humblest peasant knew what it
devolved upon him as a Hebrew to do, and was quick
and willing to show himself a loyal member of his
clan if not of his people; of the latter relation we cannot speak confidently. Surely, in view of the peril in
which some clans as Issachar, Naphtali, and Zebulun

were in the days of Sisera, the failure of Reuben, Dan, and Asher to rally to their support seems despicable. And it was with the three hundred valiant men of his own sept or clan, it appears, that Gideon had to take summary vengeance upon Midian. In this instance other septs and clans may not have been given an opportunity; still it may be questioned whether, had they had such opportunity, they would have responded with the alacrity which later historians represent them as manifesting.[1] But though the peasant's or the villager's loyalty was solely loyalty to his clan, he was in temperament socially inclined. He could not live apart from men. He did not take easily to an ascetic life; he loved the haunts of men and availed himself to the extent of his means, and even beyond, of those opportunities which were possible for coming into pleasant, social touch with life.

[1] On morality as an affair of the clan, see Budde, *The Rel. of Is. to the Ex.*, p. 33.

CHAPTER VIII

CHARACTERISTIC STORIES

" THE great value of the Book of Judges," remarks
Professor G. F. Moore in his *Polychrome Judges*, "lies
in the faithful and vivid pictures which it gives us
of this troubled and turbulent time in which historical
Israel was making." He adds, " Hardly any narrative
in the Old Testament throws more light on the social
and religious life of the ancient Israelites than the
story of Micah's idol and the migration of the Danites
(cc. xvii., xviii.)." [1] Piepenbring, in his history of the
people of Israel, has a chapter on " The Moral Life," [2]
in which he, with scarcely a remark, retells this story
and the story that follows, " The Outrage of Gibeah."
The character of these stories and their great fulness
of detail seems enough to warrant at this point a
special study of them, that their sociological data may
be looked at directly.   Such study need not prevent
our making other use of them as our consideration of
various subjects may naturally suggest.   There is the
more occasion for such study from the fact that in the
case of the first story late redactors have worked over
the material and have in so doing made numerous
additions ; and also because in the case of the second
story, similar, though more considerable, changes have

[1] Moore, *Judges*, *P.*, p. 45.　　[2] *His. du Peu. d'Is.*, p. 119 ff.

been made. Only the simpler and original form of these stories specially interests us. Upon the original form of these two and one other story we shall dwell briefly. Whatever their chronological order, now, of course, impossible to determine, we will take them in their biblical order, beginning with the story of Micah's idol and the migration of the clan of Dan.

It seems that a man in the highlands of Ephraim had a private sanctuary, in which he placed an ephod-idol and other images. Here, as in the case of Gideon (Judges viii. 27), the ephod-idol appears to have been employed in consulting the oracle of Yahweh, *i.e.*, in determining by lot which of two courses the inquirer was to pursue. It may have been a rude image of Yahweh. At first one of his sons served as priest, but later a Levite who had wandered north from Judah was easily persuaded to serve in that capacity as keeper of the sanctuary. This would not prevent Micah from officiating at ordinary sacrificial feasts. It is hardly supposable that he would have delegated such priestly and paternal functions to another. Ample arrangements were made for the maintenance of the Levite by Micah, who seems to have rejoiced in his good fortune. There appears to have been the feeling on his part that the lot could be handled by his new priestly attendant in such a way as to secure the favour of Yahweh.

Some time after this, five Danites, representatives of the different septs of the clan, came through the hills of Ephraim on their way north seeking a suitable home for their sorely straitened people.

While being entertained by Micah over night, they interviewed the Levite and got him to cast the lot, and thus determine whether success was to crown their search. Receiving an affirmative answer, they went on and explored Laish, at the sources of the Jordan, finding a quiet folk living unsuspicious of danger in peace and security. Returning, they incited their people to migrate. Six hundred warriors, armed freemen apparently, with their wives and children, presumably the major part of the clan, set out, falling upon and carrying off Micah's sanctuary, Levite and all, the man not being loath to become the priest of a clan which would be able to maintain him more generously than a single well-to-do freeman. The protests of Micah avail not. The Danites keep on their way, and, reaching Laish, overthrow it and dispossess the people whom they both spoil and slaughter. In this case we follow as reliable and as substantially true to the age the story as given in Judges, omitting only the various editorial notes of later redactors. The *naïvete* of this story is remarkable. There is no thought that this Ephraimite worship is such as can in any way be displeasing to Yahweh. The people are true to their highest conceptions of religion. On the whole, there is apparently on their part something of the same satisfaction which Micah felt when he, having got an ephod-idol for his new sanctuary, was so fortunate as to have a Levite come his way. That they were wronging the man did not seem to disturb them, for he was outside their clan, a man of Ephraim. Morality was not among the Israelites wholly a thing of the clan, though it must

have been largely so.[1] They surely would not have
violated a tribal sanctuary of Ephraim, because they
were numerically inferior to that clan. Perhaps they
would not have done so had they been superior in
point of numbers. Some reverence for holy places
of note, and possibly some sense of kinship, especially
as they were a Rachel clan, might have restrained
them. Their utter unconcern for the fate of Laish
and her people is characteristic of the time. It leads
us to surmise that the Hebrew clans when they settled in Canaan might have slaughtered with well-
nigh as bloody a hand as the priestly passages in
Joshua assert that they did, without seriously embar-
rassing compunctions. What Yahweh, their God, put
within their reach was theirs to secure and hold, regardless of the suffering it might entail upon others.
If it is said that they may have spared most of the
women and children in this instance, that, after all,
the people may not have been wholly devoted to the
sword, we can only say in reply that at the best it was
from our point of view, which, of course, could not be
theirs, an outrage and slaughter of a grim and bloody
type.

The story of the outrage of Gibeah comes to us
out of the very heart of those rough times, yet with
gleams of the dawning of a better day that was to
rise upon Israel; for that such an outrage was not

---

[1] Budde, *The Rel. of Is. to the Ex.*, p. 33.

Piepenbring very truly says, in commenting on this incident: "Ils
associent sans le moindre scrupule le vol et la piété. Ils ne trou-
vent aucune incompatibilité entre les deux."—*Histoire du Peuple
d'Israël*, p. 122.

allowed to go unpunished, argues well for the growing social consciousness of the people.[1] A Levite,
living in Ephraim, took as a concubine, probably
before going north, for he very likely originated in
the territory of Judah, a woman from Bethlehem-
Judah, who so pined for her home that she ran away.
Following, the Levite found her, as he expected to, at
her old home. A state of society that rendered it
possible for such a woman to make her way from the
highlands of Ephraim to the hill country of Judah,
could not have been wholly disorganised. There
must have been more than a semblance of law and
order, to say the least. The father-in-law of the
Levite, relieved and gratified to have him seek his
daughter, received him joyfully, and detained him as
long as possible, until near the close of the fourth
day. Setting out with his concubine and his servant,
the man passed by the city of the Jebusites and made
his way, as he pressed on, to Gibeah of Benjamin,
which he reached late in the evening. But for an old
man he might perforce have spent the night in the
public square. What this would have meant, the
sequel of the story only too clearly reveals. As it
was, a rabble of base fellows surrounded the house,
calling for the stranger, that they might vilely abuse
him. At most, their importunities and threats secured only the concubine. They so maltreated and
outraged her that she died toward morning, after
they had left. The Levite, finding her body without

[1] Moore, *Judges*, *I. C.*, p. 402 ff. ; *Judges*, *P.*, p. 92 ff. The
story as we have it does not belong to the early years of the settlement. Much of it appears to be very late.

the door, placed it upon his ass and took it home. He then cut it up and sent the pieces to the men of Ephraim and of neighbouring clans. It was enough ; the clansmen, stirred by the story of the outrage, rallied and wrought vengeance upon Gibeah. That the men of Benjamin came to the defence of Gibeah seems as improbable as that the story of the well nigh complete extermination of that clan should be regarded as veritable history. They may, it is true, have resented such interference with their jurisdiction. The fact that in Saul's day the clan of Benjamin seemed to be prosperous, and to be in no way in disfavour, may be mentioned as against the supposition that the story of the shattering of Benjamin as we have it in this narrative is true to fact. There surely is nothing in the Song of Deborah or in 1 Samuel to lead us to suppose that the clan of Benjamin was greatly reduced in numbers at this time. Indeed, quite the contrary appears to have been the fact. Saul was largely backed by his own clan, while David, after Saul had passed away, was years in getting the better of Benjamin, the one clan that clung to the House of Saul. The extent to which the story bears marks of having been worked over allows us the benefit of a doubt at this point. It is worthy of note that most of the additions are in the general style of the post-exilic writers. We must conclude that they were very late.

According to one account, the Benjaminites who were left wifeless, for the women appear to have suffered total extermination as the narrative suggests, were permitted to bear away the maidens of

Shiloh as they came forth at the feast of the vintage; according to another account, the inhabitants of Jabesh-Gilead were put to the sword and four hundred virgins who were spared were given them. Probably, both stories grew out of the effort of late editors to explain the prosperity of a clan which, according to story, had been thought to be shattered in their ancient past. The story of the rape of the virgins of Shiloh is full of local colour, and furnishes sociological data of great value, but both stories appear to be old and to emphasise characteristics of an early time. The fact that they were late as literary compositions as we now have them, does not forbid our supposing them to have had an early origin in a less finished form.

The one lesson which the outrage of Gibeah taught Israel was a lesson which they seemed not to need to learn, that the laws of hospitality were sacred and inviolable. It is probable that it was because the outrage violated their social sentiments rather than because they wished to make an example of Gibeah that they so summarily punished them. Men belonging to such a social stage do not usually inflict punishment for disciplinary purposes, as they do not trouble themselves to discover the real culprits. The innocent must suffer with the guilty. As a story revealing the social atmosphere of the time, the outrage of Gibeah has value. It should be looked at as mirroring in remarkable ways the rougher side of the life of that early period, together with some of its more hopeful features.

Our third and final story, here considered as spe-

cially characteristic of the time, belongs to the latter
part of Saul's career, though it has to do more particularly with David, who is living a semi-nomadic
life of outlawry in the south. A man by the name
of Nabal, who appears to be well-to-do, is making
merry in sheep-shearing time, after the manner of
pastoral people, to whom the season ordinarily is a
time of special festivity.[1]   David, as a sort of Bedouin
sheik who has restrained his own men, no small thing
for him to do under the circumstances, and who has
also had an eye for Nabal's welfare in other directions,
as one strong enough to protect him from the dep-
redations of roving bands, sends to him, as according to the customs of the time he had a right to do,
asking a gratuity. The ten young men sent greet
Nabal in the name of their leader, saying unto him :
" Peace be unto thee, and prosperity to thine house
and to all that thou hast. Behold our leader has
heard that the shearers are with thee. Now, thy
shepherds have been with us and we did them no
harm, neither was aught missing unto them all the
time they were in Carmel. Ask thy young men and
they will tell thee. Wherefore let us now find grace
in thy sight ; for we are come in a good day, a day
of festivity. Give, we pray thee, whatsoever cometh
to thine hand unto thy servants and to David, thy
son."

The churlish Nabal is not one to appreciate any fav-
ours shown him ; he is not minded to respond to this
very reasonable request. He can even roughly, with
words, insult the sheik and his men : " Who is David ?

[1] 1 Sam. xxv. 2 ff.   See here Smith's *Samuel*, *I. C.*

Who is this son of Jesse? There be many lawless men in these days, slaves who break away from their masters. Shall I then take my bread, and my water, and the flesh that I have provided for my shearers, and give it to men who come I know not whence?" The words are purposely made as insulting as possible.

Chagrined, David's young men return and report the interview. Now, indeed, there will be no restraining of the men, even if the sheik is minded to restrain them, but he is not. Word is passed around: "Gird ye on every man his sword." David and four hundred of his men arm themselves and sally forth, leaving two hundred to guard their stronghold and their belongings.

In the meantime, Abigail, the comely, wise, and efficient wife of the old churl,[1] has heard all that has occurred at home. She is not left in ignorance of David's chivalrous treatment, if, indeed, she was not before cognisant of it: "Behold, David sent young men out from his stronghold among the hills, out in the wilderness, to salute our master, and he flew at them and shamefully answered them. Thou knowest that David's men have been good to us. They did not in any way harm us; we missed nothing as long as we were near them shepherding our flocks. They were a wall unto us both by day and by night, all the time we were with them. Now, therefore, know and consider what you will do; for evil is assuredly determined against our master and against all his house;

[1] She was probably the younger of his wives. Such a man in those days was sure to be a polygamist.

and he is so unreasonable that one cannot advise him." There is no time for delay. Abigail must act swiftly and wisely. Two hundred loaves are quickly baked, five sheep are dressed, skins of wine are brought forth, with large quantities of corn and raisins and cakes of figs, and asses are laden therewith. The resources at the disposal of this woman, who in her own home has a position of authority and can avail herself at will of such, are ample; yet the quantities taken, though generous, are only enough to suffice for the immediate needs of David's band. It is thus that she would refresh them and predispose their sheik to listen to her words. Nabal, to be sure, is kept in ignorance, perhaps the more easily because a drunken debauch may have followed upon his dismissal of the young men. It is the fact that the action of Abigail is that of a competent woman who reveals by her act that she is not unskilled in affairs that is especially to be noted. It means much that such a woman could be conceived of, to say nothing of her being described.

The attendant servants are sent on ahead with the supplies, while Abigail makes her way tremblingly toward David. While thus going she halts by the way in a shady covert under a hill-side. David comes up with his men, cherishing his grievance and excusing himself for the vengeance which he proposes to wreak upon Nabal: "Surely in vain have I kept all that this churl hath here in the wilderness, so that nothing was missed of all that belonged to him; and now behold he hath requited me evil for good. God do so to David, and more also, if I leave of all that pertaineth unto him by the morning light so much as one male child." Abigail, so soon as she beholds David, lights off her ass, and making her way to him, prostrates herself before him upon the ground. She takes upon herself the blame for the treatment which David's men had received, admitting with perfect candour, and not without a humorous touch, the folly of her husband, and pleads for forgiveness. As a magnanimous man David vouchsafes her request, and accepting her gift, sends her back with his blessing.

Nothing is said upon her return to her carousing lord, but when in the morning she tells him all, his heart fails him, he is stricken as one who has had an apoplectic shock. Ten days thereafter he dies. Later, when David learns what has happened, he sends servants to Abigail to inform her that he proposes to wed her. Nothing loath, she hies her, with five of her damsels, to her new-found lord, not waiting for him to come to her. As a story this is not as true to the early time as that of Samson's Timnath experience; yet, as compared with the more finished prose idyl of Genesis xxiv., the wonderful story of the courtship of Rebekah, it bears the marks of an earlier hand, and presents us data that belong more surely to the early period.

These three stories which have been considered here are so characteristic of the period we are studying that they need to be read again and again until their very atmosphere is felt. It has been an effort for many undoubtedly to realise that the first is as characteristic of the time as the other two. Of the three we must give it the preference, though the others should by no means be lightly regarded. With these, others might very profitably have been studied, as, for example, the story of the taboo placed by Saul upon food, which taboo came near to being the death of Jonathan, but it seems hardly necessary to bring together here stories that elsewhere in this volume are made extensive use of in the way of illustration.

CHAPTER IX

THE RELIGION OF THE PEOPLE

THE peoples among whom these Hebrew clans dwelt were wanting in unity. There may have been a kinship of race, but religion was not among them, as among the Hebrews, the same unifying force. Not one Baal but many Baalim kept them apart as cities and separated them from the people of Yahweh. They might come together when the growth of the Hebrews seemed to imperil them; there might at least be formed now and then a confederacy of a few cities, and in a campaign like that under Sisera's leadership they might seek to humble these foreign clans, while their commercial affairs might keep them from isolating themselves from one another. Even their common worship of the various local Baalim might beget similar sentiments and might make it possible for them as individuals to feel at home in one another's cities. But as there was no national life in the true sense of the term, so there was no national God; indeed, we may say, there was no national life, because there was no one God around whom their sentiments could crystallise. The Baal of a city and its dependencies seems to have been the recognised God of the people of that particular group; as such he was worshipped as the Lord of husbandry, upon whom they depended for their

crops as agriculturalists. In the cultivation of field
and vineyard he was the power back of nature who
had it in his hands to give or to withhold, and inasmuch as they depended largely upon husbandry,
their worship as a people was chiefly a worship of
Baal and his associate Astarte. Life was, for the
most part, summed up in terms of service to these;
especially was the thought of generation associated
with them and their worship. The fruitfulness of
field and beast and man depended upon their being
propitious. All this opened the way for licentious
rites and ceremonies which at first as instituted may
have been designed to further the very ends desired
and sought, but which in time may have led, and apparently did lead, to carnivals of lust.

The Hebrew clans when they entered Canaan came
very naturally to regard the local Baalim as the proprietors of the soil, and fell into Canaanitish ways,[1]
looking to these local gods for success as agriculturalists and worshipping them; but quite apart
from this disposition to acknowledge these local
Baalim as the proprietors of the soil, and as such the
givers of the produce of the field and the vineyard,
was that necessary intercourse with them through
their relations, commercial and social, with their
neighbours. Professor Moore says very truly : " The
religious exclusiveness of the ancient world was possible only upon terms of complete non-intercourse." [2]

---

[1] Cheyne and Black, *Encyc. Bib.*, vol. i., c. 338; Hastings'
Dictionary, vol. i., p. 167 ff. ; Smith, *Rel. of the Sem.*, pp. 94 ff.,
336, etc.; Budde, *Rel. of Is. to Ex.*, chaps. i. and ii.

[2] Moore, *Judges, I. C.*, p. 83. See also Appendix VIII.

Inasmuch as the Hebrews did not isolate themselves, their intercourse with the Canaanites meant fellowship with their gods. Yahweh was their own peculiar God, and he was a God of thunder and of tempest, fierce and threatening, a war God. In times of conflict he was Yahweh of hosts, and he seemed to come up from the desert to fight for them and give them success over their enemies. They may have acknowledged their dependence upon the many local Baalim, but when it came to warfare, their confidence in their Yahweh of hosts was all-controlling and all-impelling.

As there had been in their wanderings a tent of tryst without the camp in which Yahweh was inquired of, so, it is reasonable to suppose, there were later houses of Yahweh in Bethel and in Shiloh. Perhaps in Gilgal and in other sacred places there may have been a house or shrine whither the people could go in times of perplexity. An annual feast seems to have brought many of the people together at these sanctuaries, where in the common worship of Yahweh and in a common meal they might rejoice together. Levites appear to have early come to serve at these and more private shrines. Men known as men of Yahweh rather than "Messengers of Yahweh," for this latter conception belongs to a later day, stand forth somewhat dimly as having an honoured and influential place among the members of the clans, but it is not until near the close of the period that one of these, Samuel, makes an impression upon the literature. He is to us significant, not so much for what he was as because he indicates what certain men must have been at an earlier time. These men seem to have sustained relations to individuals rather than to the clan. As such they may not have done much to bring the people together and socialise them, except where as prominent men they lived at local shrines. Whether covenants were made by worshippers among themselves and with their God is an important question that should be answered affirmatively. When so answered, the answer is seen to have an important, even vital, bearing upon the social side of the people's lives. At Shechem and at other places the Baal was known as Baal-berith, the Lord of a covenant. So Yahweh may early have been known. Such use of their God would naturally commend itself to the Hebrews when weary of war or of controversy. In their common life as Hebrews, and to considerable extent in their contact with other people, such covenants as the covenant of blood, the covenant of salt, and the threshold covenant were probably not unknown.

Images, those of Yahweh and other gods, were apparently used. Gideon makes and uses an ephod-idol, and when the men of Dan are migrating, they come upon a local shrine, only to lay hands upon it, as we have seen, and take it and all its appurtenances, including the Levite who officiated thereat, north with them.

Sacrifices were often made, not alone when domestic animals were slaughtered, but at other times, as feeling or circumstances seemed to suggest. Even human sacrifices were not unknown. The daughter of Jephthah was offered in fulfilment of a solemn vow. This is significant ; though it is mentioned in such a way as to leave the impression that members of one's family or one's clan were seldom slaughtered. Personal enemies or enemies of the clan, as, for example, captives taken in war, probably formed the major part of the victims. Abimelech so offers the seventy sons of Jerubbaal, thus avoiding the avenger of blood.

In thus considering the religion of these Hebrew clans in a general way, our chief concern is the social aspects of it. What influence had it upon the social life of the people? So far as the worship was that of Canaanite deities, it must have tended to produce friendly feelings as a rule on the part of their neighbours, especially as it usually meant the enrichment of their local shrines. This was undoubtedly their way of levying tribute upon the members of these Hebrew clans. But if there were gains, there were also disastrous consequences. The worship of female deities at these shrines, the constant association of the thought of generation with them, and the prostitution of women who served as priestesses, tended to lower socially and morally all who participated in their worship. "Of the cultus of Astarte we know comparatively little. Religious prostitution was not confined to the temple of Astarte, nor to the worship of female divinities. Num. xxv. 1–5; Amos ii. 7; Deut. xxiii. 17, 18, etc., show that in Israel similar practices infected even the worship of Yahwe. There is no doubt, however, that the cultus of Astarte was saturated with these abominations." [1]

The service of Yahweh was of a purer kind, partly

[1] G. F. M. in the Cheyne and Black, *Encyc. Bib.*, vol. i., c. 338.

because no female deity was associated with him;
though as the God of war he must often have been
thought of as cruel and bloodthirsty. Here, too, was
a real centre of social fellowship and unity which contained vast promise of good to these imperfectly
welded clans. Idols may have been used as images
of Yahweh that tended to localise him, but, after all
to the members of these clans Yahweh was one, and
as such the common property of them all. Nowhere
does this come out more clearly or more beautifully
than in the battle ode of Judges v. There is here no
abstract thought; such conceptions were far from the
author's mind; but there is a common ownership in
Yahweh, a common recognition of him, and a common praise of him. In no other passage can we get
a truer conception of what Yahweh was to these Hebrews. And it is a noteworthy fact that while he is
addressed reverently, there is revealed a familiarity of
tone and a joyousness that suggests the thought that
their religion, and their literature which was allied
closely to their religion, was a great socialiser.[1] Conduct and character may have been largely a matter of
clan loyalty, but they were what they were because of
what their God was conceived by them to be. He
was larger than clan, as he was above clan ; and so he
could inspire and gladden them. If there was not
yet a genuine affection for him, there was at least reverence and pride in him as the highest and holiest
being of whom they knew or could conceive.

[1] On the character of Yahweh in early Israel, see *Encyc. Brit.*
(Wellhausen), vol. xiii., p. 399.   On the growth in the ethical character of Yahweh worship, see Budde, *Rel. of Is. to Ex.*, p. 36 ff.

The fact that their God seemed to require of them human sacrifices need not be considered strange. To the Israelites there was nothing peculiarly revolting in such sacrifices, for they had not a profound conception of the dignity and worth of human life. The value of it, as compared with animal life did not appear to them, as it did not to other peoples of the time.

But while we admit that Yahwism was on its way toward something higher and purer, and was already a beneficent force in Israel as compared with other and more debasing types of religion, we must remember that among these Semites there were unquestionably relics of a primitive polytheism that must have held back socially the mass of the people. This is not the place to enter into a discussion of the teraphim. That they were household gods is the opinion of many. Kittel speaks of the teraphim cult as "a relic of the ancient Semitic worship of ancestors." Others, as G. F. Moore, are inclined to question whether the teraphim were ever so used. We may have to conclude that they were household idols, not necessarily used, perhaps never used, in ancestor worship, that remained from polytheistic times. So commonly were they used, and so often do we find mention of them, that we cannot forbear hoping that later research may reveal to us their real significance. If it should appear that they are relics of an earlier polytheism among the Hebrews, they are but what we might expect to find. Here, as well as at many other points in our study of the social life of the early Hebrews, it is necessary to make large use of the comparative method. Only by so doing can we understand the meagre data at our disposal.

That totemism was common in early Israel, and that it played a large part in the social life of the time, seems probable. The mere mention of it here is enough to suggest to the reader that a careful study of the religion of Israel reveals the fact that our old conceptions of the religious life of the time must be reconstructed, otherwise we cannot understand the peculiar nature of its influence upon the social life of the period. The study of totemism among other peoples, as the North American Indians and Esquimaux, is helpful here; but much more suggestive is the study of totemism among the early Arabians as brought out by W. Robertson Smith in his *Religion of the Semites*. That Israel was emerging from a totemistic stage of social life at the time of the settlement is probable; though how long the people were in ridding themselves of its thraldom, it is impossible to say. It is significant that the names of some of the clans appear to have been totem names.

CHAPTER X

IF the various Hebrew clans entered the land of Canaan at or about the same time, crossing over the Jordan from the eastern hill country, they may have been actuated by a sense of their common kinship; but so independent were certain groups of one another at the time of settlement, that it is difficult for us to believe that there was among them a real unity of purpose and of sentiment such as a pronounced national consciousness might, had it been possessed, have made possible. It has been surmised that their desert life unified Israel; even Kuenen speaks of it as making for unity, though "as a temporary co-operation." That there was a trysting-place, with the Ark as the seat of Yahweh, during their desert life appears probable; though whether it was Kadesh-barnea or some other sanctuary does not indubitably appear. It seems unreasonable to suppose that the various clans journeyed about the Arabian desert together; it is likely that they separated and wandered about for pasturage. Still, a central sanctuary would serve to unify them, though its power over the individual clans to whom their clan organisation and their common action in endeavour and in sacrifice were of supreme concern may not have been great, especially if

Yahwism was, as Budde contends, the religion of the Kenites, to which Moses introduced them. Until we know more of the religion of the Hebrews in Egypt, it is hardly safe for us to speak confidently of the unity of Israel during the bondage. Though a common oppression and consciousness of a common origin may measurably have kept them together, whether a common monotheism did, now seems questionable. That there was a sense of nationality earlier than the monarchy, and an inner unity back of the settlement, as Wellhausen thinks, we may admit, as we may also that Moses was its author. We may say with him that the basis for the unification of the tribes must certainly have been laid before the conquest of Canaan proper; but during the early part of the period of the Judges there was more to segregate the Hebrews than to unite them. The Canaanites were wanting in unity, so that only on rare occasions were the Hebrew clans forced to act together,[1] and then only a part of them at most, as in the time of Deborah.[2] The Judges as local vindicators had little need, as a rule, of a united Israel; if they could rally a few thousand clansmen, they were reasonably sure of a victory. The most conspicuous note of unity that was struck before the Philistines came in force upon the stage, was in the Song of Deborah, and, it may be, in the campaign against Sisera which it cele-

[1] *Encyc. Brit.*, vol. xiii., p. 398 (Wellhausen). "It was most especially in the graver moments of its history that Israel awoke to full consciousness of itself and of Jehovah." See also Schultz, *Old Test. Theology*, vol. i., p. 146 f.

[2] Judges v. 13–18 ; see also Judges vi. 34, etc.

brated. Here Yahweh is the God whose name forms a rallying cry.[1] That it was so, is significant. It suggests that as the Hebrews became more and more distinctively the people of Yahweh, they realised somewhat their oneness.

But nationalism, in the largest sense of the term, became a fact when the growing Philistine power threatened their enslavement and impoverishment, if not their extermination. It was the success of their enemies, and especially their capture of the Ark,[2] that stirred Israel and led them later to look for a leader. Their rallying about Saul after he had delivered Jabesh-Gilead was inevitable. There were strange vicissitudes of experience ahead ; some parts of Israel were to feel their need more than others, and the loyalty of the people was to be in proportion to the service which this man, the last of the Vindicators of Israel, was to render them ; but through the stress and the storm of the days of Saul's unhappy career there was emerging a people more conscious than their progenitors of their oneness.

The rise of prophetism, as seen in the prophetic guild which Samuel did so much to foster, further unified the people.[3] As Saul's sun declined, and as

---

[1] Moore, *Judges*, *P.*, p. 44 ; Hastings' *Dictionary*, vol. ii., p. 807 ; *Encyc. Brit.*, vol. xiii., p. 401 ; Kittel, *His. of the Hebrews*, vol. ii., p. 74 f.

[2] This loss revealed their want of unity.—Kittel, *His. of the Heb.*, vol. ii., p. 105 ff.

[3] Kuenen, *The Rel. of Is.*, vol. i., p. 317 f. ; Budde, *The Rel. of Is. to the Ex.*, pp. 90, 100 ; *Encyc. Brit.*, vol. xiii., p. 402. Wellhausen speaks here of an ecstatic group of enthusiasts provoked by Philistine invasion.

that of David rose, this movement gained impetus, so
that when long after David took Jerusalem, and by a
wise stroke of policy made it his Royal City, Ephraim
and Judah were apparently becoming one people
and were, in becoming so, drawing all Israel after
them. The movement was from the first uneven.
The progress at times was rapid, as at other times it
was slow, with set-backs that were discouraging ; but,
on the whole, the political and social evolution was
somewhat in the direction of a unity of thought
and sentiment. There were differences enough in
the location of the various groups to have led to a
somewhat different type of social life had it not been
for this growing nationalism ; but this unification
meant oneness of social life as did the slow disintegration of the clan organisations following upon the
settlement. At no time during the period here
treated could an Israelite of one clan have felt himself when among the members of another clan a perfect stranger, but there may have been such differences of sentiment and of custom as to have kept
such a man from feeling at home. Until the time of
the monarchy the clan or city must have meant more
to the individual Hebrew than the larger social body.
We may easily believe that to many of these various
clans their social relations with certain Semites who
were not Hebrews meant more than similar relations
with those outside of their own clan who were Hebrews.

PART II

THE TIME OF THE MONARCHY

CHAPTER I

FOR convenience we may speak of the social life treated in this second part as lived under the monarchy, though the Hebrews did not, even under David and Solomon, become one. The chroniclers of the time speak of Israel and Judah near the close of David's life, after he had vainly tried to unify them, although often showing an unwise partiality for his own clan. Though the line of cleavage did not appear as markedly in Solomon's day, the unification of the people of the north and the south had not yet been effected. It takes more than a generation or two, even where the circumstances are peculiarly favourable, to amalgamate peoples having a divergent ancestry and divergent traditions, as well as a somewhat different environment. The literature of the two peoples reveals in part their differences; while the location of the northern clans kept them in closer touch with outside life, as it also enabled them to spread down into the rich plains, as they got the better of their neighbours, largely through their numerical increase and their superior enterprise and thrift. Judah meanwhile was left for the most part to her barren hills, upon which the people were forced to maintain themselves by means of their flocks and herds, or by the absorption of near-by nomadic peoples, as the Calebites and the Ken-ites, as well as the Jebusites and others, among whom they had come as intruders. The ease with which the northern clans swung off by themselves under Jeroboam reveals their want of oneness with Judah, to whom they must have been in point of numbers largely superior. To bring about the sev-erance of the outward bond of unity, there was little need of the traditional stupidity and obstinacy of Rehoboam.

But though up to the time of the final break-up of the Northern Kingdom, in 722 B.C., by Sargon of Assyria, the monarchy was dual, and though the Hebrews of the two parts of Canaan had their separate lines of kings and were much of the time little inclined to a mutual interchange of the courtesies of life, they may never-theless be studied as one people from the stand-point of the sociologist. It was not until wealth began to pile up under Jeroboam II., through foreign conquests and the widening industrial life of his people, that the type of social life changed radically in the north as compared with the south. Even then the proud and vain inhabitants of Jerusalem seem to have vied, with some appearance of success, with the wealthy nabobs of Samaria. Besides, after all, the richer fruitage in the realm of literature and religion which has come to us from the Hebrews is in itself our warrant for a study of their social life in its entirety, regardless of geographical boundaries. Such a study need not conceal the social differences in ideals and in life, for the emphasising of some of the more pronounced of

these will but add to the picturesqueness and interest
of our narrative.

The problem which the question of sources for the
social life of this period presents is most intricate.
The difficulty of the problem is in this instance enhanced by reason of the fact that so much in the way
of textual criticism of the Old Testament remains to
be done. Had we in hand the volume on *The
Kings*, by the Rev. Francis Brown, D.D., and that
on *The Chronicles*, by the Rev. Edward L. Curtis,
D.D., both of which volumes are sure to maintain
unimpaired the reputation of the series of which they
are to constitute a part, our labour would be materially
reduced. As it is, the author has been thrown back
upon himself, and has been forced to do much of his
grubbing in the text unaided. This accounts largely
for the paucity of references to first-class authorities
in this part as compared with Part I. of this volume.
Few textual helps of a high order as we possess
here there are some that deserve special mention.
Smith's *Samuel*, already named in connection with
Part I.; Budde's *The Books of Samuel*, in *The
Polychrome Hebrew Text;* Kittel's *The Chronicles*, in
the same text; Driver's *Introduction to the Literature
of the Old Testament;* G. A. Smith's *Isaiah*, and his
first volume in *The Twelve Prophets;* and Dillmann's
Genesis are invaluable; while throughout, but espe-
cially in connection with the Books of Samuel, the
Septuagint cannot be dispensed with.

But what of the sources which must be studied by
the student of the English Bible with such helps as
he may at present be able to command ? How ex-

tensive are they, and of just how much critical value
as furnishing tolerably reliable data of a sociological
character? Such questions must be faced at the out-
set by the student of this period. Upon the answer
which he gives, depends the value very considerably
of the work done. Unless the student be possessed
of considerable critical acumen, he must fail. He
should accept only the most careful analysis of the
strata of the different historical books and the legal
codes, and should admit as literature contemporary
thereto only that which is indubitable. Having, however, done this, he may to a considerable extent ignore the finer points as to dates; for, inasmuch as the
period covered is nearly four centuries, and the social
life is to be looked at in the large, he cannot go far
astray in marshalling his data. Rejecting all that
belongs to the earlier period, he must with as firm a
hand set aside all that shows unmistakable marks of
the Deuteronomist and Priestly Writer. Within
these limits he has considerable freedom, and may
advance with reasonable confidence. For example,
accepting the J and E patriarchal stories of Genesis,
as now we are bound to do, as late, stories that as literature were closely related to the old sanctuaries of
Shechem, Bethel, Hebron, and Beer-sheba, belonging
to the ninth or, possibly, the eighth century B.C., he
may use, at least in an illustrative way, their sociological data. So, too, after he has for his purposes
rejected the few parts of 2 Samuel, which belong to the men of the Deuteronomic or Priestly
Schools, though he may feel that the stories look
very much like an attempt of a writer subsequent to

Solomon who wished to exalt him in the eyes of later generations, still he must admit that these stories furnish valuable material for reconstructing, in a tentative way at least, a fascinating picture of the social life of the time. If his attempt prove a failure, the fault is his own.

Let us look, then, without going into any of the finer questions of textual criticism, at our broad field, and view in a general way the rich mass of material which the scholarship of our day puts at our disposal. We have 2 Samuel, which begins with the death of Saul and the crowning of David at Hebron. How rich this is in sociological data only he can know who has read it critically under the lead of such careful students as Wellhausen, Budde, Driver, and H. P. Smith. Parts of 2 Samuel must be handled carefully, if not ruled out altogether, because they belong to a date so late that the writer's knowledge of the social life of the time under consideration must have been fallible. Wholly so it may not have been. Take, for example, the men belonging to the Deuteronomic School. Legitimate worship in Solomon's day and thereafter, was in their thought at one central sanctuary. In alluding to the high places prior to Solomon, or in condemning the worship which, during later centuries, was common thereat, the Deuteronomists may help us to understand them, for they were still in existence in their day, and were so common that they could not speak of them without doing so out of the fulness of their personal knowledge, though revealing at the same time their strong bias and proneness to mis-

interpret history in the interests of their higher
moral ideals. We have little from their hand in
2 Samuel. We have more of theirs in 1 Samuel,
which, though belonging in its more reliable portions to our first period, the time of the vindicators, may here be used illustratively to a considerable
extent, because it has to do with a time so near the
establishment of the monarchy. But with even less
favour must we look upon any priestly or other exilic
parts of the book, as, for example, chapter seven, the
famous Messianic passage, and the so-called last
words of David, which are even more innocent of any
knowledge of the supposed author and his time, than
are the so-called last words of Jacob and of Moses,
and the psalm of Hannah of their supposed authors
and their time. Such sociological data as they give
us, and this may, when properly understood, be extremely valuable, can be used by the student only
where it belongs, unless, indeed, he wishes to stultify
his historical sense.

The Books of the Kings down to the time of Josiah,
641 B.C., that is, to 2 Kings, xxi. 26, must be largely
used by us. Here again we have a rich mine in
which to delve, though not as rich as 2 Samuel,
for proportionally it covers a much longer period,
and is to a considerable extent fragmentary. Here,
however, the Deuteronomist revels,[1] consigning to his
limbo royalty and people in a wholesale way, because,
forsooth, they had used most freely for religious and
social purposes the high places which were well nigh
the only centres of the Yahweh cult known to them,

[1] Hastings' *Dictionary*, vol. ii., p. 859 ff.

and which, despite their abuses, and especially their sensual excesses, had not without good reasons endeared themselves to the Hebrews during the long centuries in which they had used them.   To the Deuteronomist the work of the great Elijah had counted for little or nothing.   These high places continued, and they were evil and only evil in their influence. What they were to him they must, in his thought, always have been.   On the other hand, the elaborately constructed temple described for us in 1 Kings has absolutely nothing to do with the social life of the people of the period here treated.

Similarly the Books of the Chronicles down to Josiah's day, that is, to 2 Chronicles xxxiii. 25, should be used, yet with decreasing confidence, for here we encounter the Priestly School at every step of the way, a School which was superior to all others in the freedom with which it worked over historical documents.   The desire to advance a reform could not be pleaded by them as an excuse ; rather was the aim that of exalting the temple and the priestly class, though even here in the thought of the School the incomparable Yahweh, the God of the heavens and the earth, might be honoured.   The patient study of certain portions of The Chronicles, especially the drier statistical portions, brings to light some data that are not to be ignored, as, for example, the fact that the worship of Baal and Astarte played a more important part in the life of the people during the days of Saul and David than the Books of Samuel, as we now have them, would lead us to surmise.

Apart from these professedly historical works, we

have the J and E narratives of Genesis and of other parts of the Hexateuch. The most rewarding portions of these narratives are those found in Genesis, especially in the patriarchal stories[1] and the Blessing of Jacob. The social ideals and religious practices, the traditions and the customs, of the people in the ninth and eighth centuries, come so strikingly to the surface of these narratives that when read as these much misunderstood parts of the Old Testament should be read, they become marvellously illuminating and inspiring. They present to us, however, in certain portions, as in the unblushing, though unrebuked, disposition of Jacob to overreach, and in the economic and social policy of Joseph among the Egyptians, ideals that the best men of the eighth century, as Amos and Isaiah, could not heartily endorse. Among other parts of the Hexateuch, the Book of the Covenant, Ex. xx. 23–xxiii. 33, the first legal code of the Hebrews, belongs here. Attention should also be given to the J and E narratives of Exodus and Numbers, especially the parts relating to the Exodus, the story of " a rebellion of laymen against the civil authority," the account of Israel at Kadesh and their journeyings thence to the plains of Moab, and " the history of Balaam." [2] Small parts of Joshua appear to belong here ; so, also, to go outside the Hexateuch, do considerable portions of the Judges. It should, of course, be recognised that the larger part of this book belongs to the literature of this

[1] See Appendix VII.

[2] Driver, *Intro. to Lit. of O. T.*, p. 55 ff., 1st ed.; p. 60 ff. 8th ed.

period, though largely, yet cautiously, used by us in connection with our study of the social life of the Hebrew people prior to the monarchy, because the stories, or folk-tales, have to do with that time.

As we come down into the eighth century, there is a class of literature, entirely different from any we meet prior to this time, which comes into our hands, with a mass of data that is almost wholly sociological. The great names of Amos, Hosea, Isaiah, and Micah rise before us in a sublimely stirring way. Perhaps no one can so appreciate the moral ideals and the unselfish religious enthusiasm of these wonderful teachers as he who comes up to them from a careful study of the social life of the Hebrews during the centuries which separated Saul's day from theirs. Deutero-Isaiah can be explained, the Book of Job is not unaccountable, the richest of the devotional literature of the Psalms discovers to us the soil out of which it grew; but what shall we say of these men, who, if they seemed in their own eyes to have failed, became an inspiration to all who cherish high ambitions? We may speak of the high-souled, adorable Jesus as the great contradiction of all history, so utterly at variance does he seem to us to be with the life of his time; but we may not forget Amos, the herd of Tekoa, Hosea, the heart-distraught preacher of the long-suffering Yahweh, nor the more finished and cultured Isaiah and Micah. The social life of a people among whom such men sprang up could not have been altogether bad. Perhaps in some directions our ideas of it need rectification. Certainly the material gleaned in the literature already mentioned must find in the literary remains of these men, the earliest of the written prophets, invaluable supplementation. We shall prize their aid all the more if we reflect that it was nearly a century ere such prophetic voices were again heard.

CHAPTER II

FROM the beginning of this period on, the Hebrews appear to have had little trouble with the Canaanites. They may still in many regions have had to hew their own wood and draw their own water ; but they were now, especially in the south, fast absorbing the old Canaanitish stock. The Books of Samuel which have to do professedly with all Israel, though they, in fact, deal principally with David's own clan, mention the Amorites only twice and the Canaanites but once. The Books of the Kings have scarcely more to say of them. It is evident that in Solomon's day the process of absorption, while far from complete in the lowlands, and particularly in the north, was fast going on. The Hebrews could now begin to think of the land as theirs. Centuries of occupancy enabled them to regard it as in some real sense their fatherland, the home of their mythical progenitors. Though they might be spoken of by their neighbours as " Outlanders," or " Hebrews," their grip had so tightened that they could speak of the land as Yahweh's. If in their eyes he as their God had not wholly usurped Baal, if the proprietorship was still a divided proprietorship, the thought was at least an advance upon the older thought of the distant Sinai as the home of

Yahweh. For that matter, all along there had been a contradiction in their thought of Yahweh's abiding-place, for to most of them the Ark was Yahweh's seat. It seems at times as though they identified it with their God, so that the loss of it was temporarily the loss of him.[1] It is probable that in the north the problem of getting the better of the Canaanites and absorbing them had to be faced a century longer than it had in the south. Granting this, we may still declare that the environment of the social life of the people as a whole had changed, and that they had come into closer touch with the world without.[2] The great nations were for a considerable time to leave them singularly alone, perhaps because, on the whole, they despised them;[3] but when the propitious moment came, they were to step in and demand tribute. Till then the lesser highways, as that trodden by Ehud when he went with his gift-bearers to Eglon of Moab, were not to be traversed by such agents save as coming from some near-lying foreign people, they should bring their forced gratuities to the Hebrews.

Beginning with David himself, we find traces of foreign relations and alliances through marriage or through some simple form of covenant. In the harem of this king were several wives of foreign

[1] Indeed, every *maṣṣēbah*, or pillar, set up and anointed was regarded as Yahweh's dwelling-place.—Gen. xxviii. 22, etc.; Hastings' *Dic.*, vol. i., p. 75 f.

[2] Budde, *Rel. of Is. to the Ex.*, p. 114; Wellhausen, *Encyc. Brit.*, vol. xiii., p. 405 f.

[3] See, however, 1 Kings xiv. 25.

birth, as there were also concubines from Jebus and
other peoples than his own Judahites. Absalom was
a son of Maacah, the daughter of Talmai. It was to
his maternal grandfather he fled after he slew Amnon.
Bathsheba, the mother of Solomon, had for her first
husband a Hittite, a foreigner in David's service.
A critical study of the text leads us to surmise that
the reputed number of Solomon's wives and concubines may be materially reduced; but that he contracted several foreign matrimonial alliances, there
seems little reason for doubting. The mother of his
son and successor, Rehoboam, was, as we know, an
Ammonitess. If in the beginning of the days of the
monarchy, in what was after all its day of small
things, this could be, we ought to be prepared to read
of such a marriage as that of Ahab to Jezebel at a
much later day.

But not alone in these, but also in other and more
notable ways, the Hebrews came to feel themselves
to be a part of a larger world than their own. As
their nomadic pursuits broadened into other forms
of industrial life, they became of consequence com-
mercially to the nations about them. This at least
is clear from the stories of the relations which David
and Solomon sustained to Hiram of Tyre, that between the Phœnicians and the Hebrews of the time
of the monarchy there was considerable commercial
activity.   It was to foreign courts refugees fled.
Hadad of Edom went to Egypt to avoid Solomon.[1]
Thither fled Jeroboam, who had been at the head of
the forced labour of Solomon in the north, who as a

[1] 1 Kings xi. 17.

capable, energetic man was destined to divide the kingdom with his son.[1] Later we have an early attempt at extradition, though in this instance, as is often the case to-day under similar circumstances, the man was in hiding at home.[2] Peoples seem to have had at times streets of their own in foreign cities, and trade tended more and more to assume international proportions.

Small neighbouring peoples fell at first into the lap of Judah; but after the first century Moab and Ammon seem to have come under the sway of the stronger Northern Kingdom. Judah had quite enough to do to keep the Edomites up to their obligations as a tributary people. Syria found it to her advantage at times to cultivate friendly relations with both North and South Israel; covenants were made with them; at other times she devastated with fire and sword their territory. With the exception of the days of the greatest ruler the Northern Kingdom ever had, Jeroboam II., the closing century of the life of that kingdom was unsettled by the frequent Syrian invasions; while the Southern Kingdom, besides suffering at the hand of Syria, had also, after the fall of Samaria, to purchase exemption of Assyria by a tribute that must have about exhausted the financial resources of the state. Yet, despite all this, the relations sustained to other peoples must for the most part have been fairly amicable. And the influence of these different peoples upon Israel, though largely unrecognised at the time, and still more difficult to

---

[1] 1 Kings xi. 40.

[2] A part of the time at least.—1 Kings xviii. 10; cf. xvii. 3.

measure now, must have been considerable. If in the earlier time they had not been isolated, surely now they were not, situated as they were on or near the great caravan routes east and west, north and south, and within reach of the mighty armies which swept up and down the maritime plain to the west of them. The Hebrews were within the radius of influence of Phœnicia, Egypt, Babylon, and Greece. Tradition has it that they spoiled the Egyptians ere they came forth to set up a civic life of their own. The student of their life from the days of David onward is compelled to acknowledge that they continued to borrow, and that the whole ancient world became their creditors.[1] This conclusion thus forced upon us, coincides, fortunately, with our present understanding of national indebtedness.

It does not devolve upon us to set forth here the special ways in which this influence was most potent. Probably in the realm of industry including the arts, especially literature, it was no more powerful during this period than in the realm of religion; though the Persian influence was not strongly felt until after the Captivity. One cannot read, even in a cursory way, the J narrative as it is found in the Hexateuch without becoming aware of this. It is the Babylonian that here by his cosmogony and in other ways makes his influence felt. Foreign worship was, as we know, common throughout this period. The worship of Baal and Astarte clung with peculiar pertinacity to the north. Whether other foreign cults rooted themselves deeply in the life of the people may be ques-

[1] Wellhausen, *Encyc. Brit.*, vol. xiii., p. 405 ff.

tioned. It is probable that the star-gazing of the society belles of Jerusalem, a Babylonian importation, was, like similar attempts to acclimate foreign cults, in the nature of a fad, as was charioteering in the capital in the days of Absalom and Adonijah. While not attempting to estimate the amount of foreign influence, we may safely say it was unquestionably large ; though we are mainly interested in calling attention to the more patent fact that the environment of Israel had changed as they had passed out of the days of their old vindicators, when life was still largely nomadic and patriarchal, into the time of the monarchy, when Israel entered upon a stage of society which, with its many large proprietors and its overlords, or kings, was essentially feudalistic. To one thoroughly conversant with the social life in England from the days of the Saxon Heptarchies down to the time of King John, many fascinating parallels occur as he enters into the life of the Hebrews of the monarchy. Widely separated as were the two peoples in point of time they were yet essentially one in many of the characteristic features of their social life.

And if the outward environment had changed, the inner, or local, environment had also changed. Without anticipating what we shall have to say in our next chapter on the passing of the clan and the growth of the monarchy, we may here call attention to the fact that this internal change in the body politic, slow as it was in making itself felt, was nevertheless great. We had occasion in Part I. to note that the so-called Judges were, at the most, local vindicators, not rulers, who exercised for long periods, and over the whole people, judicial functions, and who controlled at the same time, with firm hand, their domestic affairs and foreign policy. The absurdity of the supposition of later centuries that they were such, is now, as we earlier contended, apparent enough. The Hebrews passed out of the days of their vindicators into the time of the monarchy, and in doing so greatly changed the internal framework of their social life; that is, the local and internal environment of the smaller aggregations altered materially, while the life as a whole found itself very differently circumstanced. In the ruling house the people discovered a new centre about which, to a greater or less extent, proportionate to its character and achievements, thought, interest, and affection could crystallise. Though the monarch might be weak, the influence of the Court would make itself widely, and often disastrously, felt ; and generally quite as widely if the ruler was weak. By one of the chroniclers, to whose narrative 1 Samuel ix.–x. 13 belongs, it is made to appear that both Samuel and Yahweh are desirous that Saul shall be anointed and raised to the rank of vindicator ; by the other, to whom the widely divergent eighth chapter owes its origin, Yahweh is said to be offended and Samuel to be extremely displeased with the people for desiring a king like the surrounding nations. Neither chronicler is wholly wrong. Monarchy, in such a stage of society as that into which they were passing, has its uses as it has also its disadvantages and its perils. But the change was made, though in the making of it, Saul but prepared the way for another better fitted for leadership. The change, which was only partial and tentative in Saul, came about more surely, yet slowly, after the crowning of David at Hebron. The student of the life of the time has to reckon with it in endeavouring to picture to himself the social side of the people's life. Henceforth there was to be a king somewhere among them as Hebrew clans or tribes. The monarchy was to be recognised, supported, and to some extent deferred to. Life was, therefore, to be more or less moulded thereby. Socially and industrially it was to make itself felt ; in just what ways we are not now prepared to say. Only a close study of the social life of the people during this period will render this apparent.

CHAPTER III

THE PASSING OF THE CLAN

THE life of the Hebrews prior to the establishment of the monarchy was, as we have seen, largely vested on both its civil and its social side in the clan, the free citizens of which determined, in accordance with ancient customs, matters of general concern. Under the rule of kings things changed and the clan fell more and more into the background as a vital factor in the social life of the people, while the civic affairs which were not arranged by the crown were left principally to the sheiks or free citizens of the various cities.[1] That this change was gradual, the fragmentary chronicles of the time reveal in many incidental hints and allusions. Not only were minor matters, as the securing of blood-revenge, where the immediate relatives for any reason shrank from demanding it, looked after by sept or clan, but for a considerable period more important matters were still in the hands of these septs and clans. Besides, the sheiks, or elders, as we persist in calling them, were frequently mentioned as being consulted or as coming to the front and taking things into their hands in times of grave concern.[2] In the days of Eli the matter of taking the Ark to battle in their cam-

[1] Wellhausen, *Eneyc. Brit.*, vol. xiii., p. 409.

[2] Kittel, *His. of Heb.*, vol. ii., p. 299 f. The prominence of the sheiks in the J and E narratives of the Exodus should be noted.

paign against the Philistines had been decided by them. Long afterward Abner communicated with them when he wanted to carry North Israel over to David. To the sheiks David himself often deferred, as at times, bidden or unbidden, these men came forward to council him. Absalom allied himself with the sheiks, and they shared with him the responsibilities which he had assumed in taking things into his own hands. David's appeal to the sheiks of Judah when he sent to them, after the overthrow of Absalom, to ascertain why they had not taken action in the matter of reinstating him, is significant. The freemen of Judah were still able to come together, if they so desired, in clan assembly for the purpose of general action. Similarly, Solomon had to do with the sheiks. The chroniclers speak of frequent conferences. Here the men consulted, as may have been very frequently the case in his father's day, were probably those of Jerusalem. Geographical location then, as has so often been the case in other lands during later centuries where the representative principle was partially recognised, largely determined the extent and character of such influence; but the mere fact that it had a place, is what we would here emphasise. Its range must have been considerable. Even such a self-reliant, aggressive man as Ahab, backed as he was by one of the most energetic women of his time, is said to have conferred with his city freemen in an affair that seemed to all of special concern.[1] That he never again deferred to them is utterly improbable.

[1] 1 Kings xxi. 8 ff.

All this, if we have not before noted it, may strike us as strange, accustomed as we have been to regard the Hebrew monarchy as absolute; but that this should have been so ought not to surprise us if we have noted the fact that there were many in those times who as large proprietors were very comfortably circumstanced. We come frequently upon men possessed of the means of Nabal, the Carmelite, without his well-known churlishness and parsimoniousness. The men who so royally received and supplied David over in the east Jordan region when he fled from Absalom, Barzilli, Shobi, and Machir, were men who had their counterparts in a large class on the west side, as also on their own.[1] Such large free proprietors are everywhere to be met in those times. Even Ziba, a feudal tenant or dependent of the House of Saul, could generously remember David as he was setting out, taking to him as he did a hundred loaves of bread, a hundred cakes of dried figs and the same of raisins, together with a skin of wine and two saddled asses.[2] This man appears almost invariably in the narratives of his time with his fifteen sons and his twenty slaves. Shimei, who manifested a different disposition in his attitude toward his royal master in distress, is able to muster and take with him a thousand Benjaminites, an adroit move on his part, when he with great show of obsequiousness goes down to the Jordan at a later day to seek restitution to favour.[3] He disappears from sight in the days of Solomon, after having given offence by going beyond

[1] 2 Sam. xvii. 27 ff.   [2] 2 Sam. xvi. 1 ff.
[3] 2 Sam. xix. 16 f.

the walls of Jerusalem, where he is kept in ward, in search of two runaway slaves.[1] Naboth was a man of enough consequence to venture to refuse Ahab his heart's desire; and though he had later to fall by reason of the perfidy of the King and his wife, he fell not without the approval of the very class of freemen to whom he himself belonged. Such free proprietors as we thus come upon so often in the chronicles of the time were men who would guard most sacredly old customs, and, clinging tenaciously to their rights as clansmen, would reluctantly yield to the royal prerogative.

That the clans gave way slowly, while the monarchy as slowly grew in favour, appears in other ways than those already mentioned. The difficulty with which David and Solomon held their thrones in the face of different aspirants to the royal dignity, is in evidence on the point under consideration. Several attempts were made to unseat David. The war in which Abner was a leading spirit, if indeed he was not wholly responsible for the movement, Ishbaal being weak and incompetent, was virtually a revolt against the expectations and pretensions of David. Had Abner been supported by the other clans as he was by Benjamin, the only clan that ever manifested much interest in the House of Saul, David must have gone down ingloriously. Absalom failed more through want of character and ordinary shrewdness than through want of support on the part of the people; while poor Sheba was backed by his own clan only.

[1] 1 Kings ii. 39 ff.

North Israel during all the days of David and Solomon was waiting for its man. It had nurtured in its liberty-loving towns and municipalities loyal free citizens, but it had trained no one man for the task of organisation and leadership. In David, on the other hand, Judah had found one who in the school of adversity had received the needed discipline. But if the people of the north submitted to the rule of Jeroboam and his successors, they certainly did not reveal any great affection for royalty. Their traditional love of liberty was too deep-seated to allow any royal house to hold them long in subjection.

Solomon's reign was not apparently as peaceful as in retrospect it seemed to priestly narrators. Some of the men who in those days sat under their own vine and fig-tree probably kept their weapons of war within easy reach. We may not follow the Deuteronomist to his conclusions here, but we may accept his admission that there was more or less unpleasantness in his reign and that the art of warfare was not forgotten in Israel.

Evidence of another kind appears in the character of the actual functions of kings and in their position as overlords possessed of a large bodyguard or small standing army. They, as David's seasoned soldiers, though few in number, on more than one occasion vanquished the raw levies opposed to them. The pomp and glitter of royalty, though on a miniature scale, made itself felt upon many. Mothers of kings as queens regent added to the glory of the throne, especially if they were of distinguished foreign extraction. The King was not, it may be, always

named by his father or predecessor, and may not
always have been proclaimed or acclaimed king by
the people, though they might not fail to greet him
with the customary salutation : "Let the King live."
Primogeniture did not hold. The length of the
Davidic line itself reveals the fact that kings usually
chose their stronger and more competent sons to this
office, as the records actually reveal that they did.
But that the King when chosen, and however chosen,
was anointed and crowned we know, and that he
maintained for those times and the people over whom
he reigned considerable state, we also know. We
trust it was the precious stone taken from the crown
that had been lifted from the head of Milcom, the
god of Ammon, that, put in David's crown, was worn
by him rather than the enormous crown itself, which,
according to the chronicler, was so heavy as to crush
any but a giant, and such even as to add to a giant's
traditional self-conceit. In the size of the King's
royal residences, in his large retinue of servants, in
his great harem of comely women brilliantly clad,
and in other ways he appealed to his people. Large
proprietors might vie with him to some extent, but
they were probably willing that he should lead, and
sometime, it may be, were fearful of incurring his
jealousy. Then, too, the King surrounded himself
with civil functionaries, men whose duty it was as a
sort of cabinet or council to assist and advise in the
conduct of the affairs of state. There was the chief
of the army, and sometimes the head of the bodyguard as distinct from the general-in-chief, a head
of the forced labour, a treasurer, a recorder or private

secretary, and a scribe. Chroniclers and men of reputed wisdom adorned the Court by their occasional presence, if they were not in constant attendance; while princes and sons of rivals, as hostages, sat at the royal board.

The judicial functions of the King are not to be overlooked. These were of pre-eminent importance. As the chief-justice the King was the final court of appeal. If these duties added greatly to the burdens of his position, they also served to magnify him in the eyes of his people, and made it possible for a king of judicial temper to strongly mould the social life of his subjects. The most serious charge that could be brought against David as he advanced in years was that he neglected his judicial duties. If the King failed here, there was none who could step in and make good his dereliction.

This subject ought not to be dismissed without reference to the chroniclers, who, for reasons of their own, saw fit to keep thought of their clans before the people. Perhaps we have here evidence of a negative sort in favour of the growing influence of the monarchy both north and south, though we quite as surely find evidence that the clan as a clan had come far short of being relegated to desuetude. In the so-called Blessing of Jacob which belongs to this period, its date being subsequent to the time of Solomon, appear distinct tribal demarcations and considerable practically independent tribal life.[1] Reuben, the first-born, the tribe that may at one time, as Dillmann

[1] Even in the later "Blessing of Moses," this is still true of the tribes.

thinks, have had the hegemony, is spoken of as preeminent, though at the same time recognised as unstable and lawless. It is rebuked for immoral customs or practices which the other tribes could not sanction. Thus we see that though this tribe in the days of the chronicler showed signs of disintegration, it was still powerful. Of Judah, on the other hand, the author of the poem speaks in such terms of praise as to reveal the fact that the Blessing of Jacob is a part of the J narrative of the Hexateuch. The reference to the sceptre and the ruler's staff as belonging to Judah and to "the obedience of the people" as his, though in striking contrast with the words concerning fruitful Joseph, yet reveal that the latter tribe was independent of the former. With fewer strokes the other tribes are pictured for us in such a way as to leave the impression that when the writer sketched them they were far from having surrendered all their rights and privileges as separate clans.

A somewhat similar impression is to be reached from reading critically the patriarchal narratives as writings which have largely to do with peoples without, and clans among the Hebrews, though here, as we might expect, while other tribes are frequently spoken of, Judah and Joseph stand out most prominently. The distance of the clans which were located beyond Esdraelon would help to exclude them from the thought of chroniclers of Ephraim and Judah; but this would also be favourable to their retention of most of their clan traditions and customs. These clans might render some sort of homage to the great tribe of Joseph; but the wholesale surrender of clan rights would not be made—far from it. Probably the fact that the reigning houses subsisted principally upon forays upon alien peoples would keep down considerably the demands made upon such clans save those for military service, and here there was always the expectation of rich spoil to lure them into doing the bidding of royalty. Still, the roving nomadic life was one thing, and the settled life another, especially as these clans as settled under the monarchy no longer took the initiative in war, and were forced to leave foreign affairs generally to their kings. The central power determined for them their foreign policies and left them at most little more than their own local affairs to manage. The comparative infrequency with which other tribes than those of Judah and Joseph are mentioned in the literature of the period does not argue the utter breakdown of their clan life, as the fact that northern clans are spoken of even by the northern chroniclers as "Israel" as a rule after the establishment of a kingly seat in the north does not. Yet we must admit that the clans as real centres of the larger life of the people faded with the centuries into insignificance, while the reigning houses became more powerful. That the prophets of the eighth century knew little of clan life seems evident. They have to do with peoples, with nations. A man's genealogy was still in his tribe ; his actual life was in Israel or in Judah.

CHAPTER IV

THE FAMILY AND THE HOME

WE have to account for the growing favour with which the monogamous family was regarded during this period.[1] A plurality of wives had been the rule among the Hebrews as nomads. Even during the age of the Vindicators, as we have seen, men who were so circumstanced as to be able to maintain more than a single wife were polygamists. Yet in process of time, during the period of the monarchy, if not earlier, monogamy came quite markedly into favour, if not with the ruling classes, at least among many of the people and among some who exerted a potent influence. The J and E narratives of the Hexateuch, which we here need to remind ourselves were not the work of individuals but of schools or centres of thought, in idealising their past, do so in such a way as to leave upon their readers the impression that monogamous marriages were to be preferred. Men like Adam, Noah, Isaac, and Joseph appear as the husbands of single partners. A beautiful idyl is that of the courtship of Rebekah, out of which narrative much of the beauty would have gone had the writer spoken in the same breath near the close of Isaac as taking

[1] Kittel, *His. of the Hebrews*, vol. ii., p. 298; Wellhausen, *Encyc. Brit.*, vol. xiii., p. 408.

to himself other wives of the daughters of the land.
It is true that certain of the patriarchs, as Abraham
and Jacob, are spoken of naturally as possessed of
more than one wife as well as concubines; but Abraham marries Keturah after Sarah's death, and Jacob
has Leah deceitfully given him to wife, a woman he
does not want, so that nothing is left to him but to
marry as quickly as he may Rachel, the woman whom
he ardently loves.   Besides, we are not to overlook
the fact that the writers of these narratives do bring
out most unpleasantly the strifes and jealousies with
which the harems of these patriarchs were rife.   The
general impression left upon the mind of the reader,
and probably designedly so left, was in favour of
monogamy.

It must in those days have become very evident to
thoughtful minds that polygamy was less suited to
a settled than a nomadic life.   As nomads there had
not only been an excuse but even evident necessity
for it; as city dwellers they found for it less occasion.   A single woman might now support herself by
honest industry without becoming a part of the harem
of some free citizen.   Nevertheless, polygamy was
slow in yielding, and could have yielded but partially
to monogamy during this period.   Elkanah appears
as the husband of two wives, though the stories
which were circulated concerning his family revealed
the unhappy state of things that existed all too often
in the homes of those times where there was a plurality of wives.   Rulers like David and Solomon set
for their people an example in this direction which,
taken with its sequels of jealousy, lust, and murder,

must have led many to think seriously, though perhaps to little purpose. When we come into the days
of the literary prophets we have no longer doubt as
to the exaltation of monogamy as an ideal, though we
are loath to believe it was widely practised even then,
save where economic reasons necessitated it. It was
in accordance with primitive ideas that the Book of
the Covenant should guard the rights of concubines
who might as bondwomen be purchased, only to be
put away later by their husbands. Such a woman
could not be sold to a strange people ; opportunity
was to be given to those who had sold her to redeem
her. Marriage was still largely a matter of barter.
The man wedding a virgin must not only remember
the bride with some gift that would gratify her, but
he must also see that the father or eldest brother, if
the father was not living, be generously remembered.
Leah and Rachel, according to story, had indignantly
reminded their father that he had sold them, yet the
servant of Abraham had given to the brother and
mother of Rebekah precious things before he had
brought her forth from Aram. Probably concubines,
who were usually female slaves bought for the purpose of serving in the home, or captives of war, and
who were made to rear children to their masters, took
very frequently the place of other wives than a first.
Common as slavery was, and much as women were
used for work long since thought to belong to men,
the number of homes without concubines, save among
the poor, must have been few. Throughout the
period they are often mentioned ; yet there were
female slaves who had husbands of their own, as the

Book of the Covenant reveals, but these were slaves of one and the same master.

Old marriage customs survived. The husband still brought his bride to his own or to his father's house, where a feast was prepared for his male friends. Ordinarily a week was given over to the occasion, during which there were gross excesses in eating and drinking. The tent of the bridegroom was pitched upon the roof, a custom which, as Dr. H. P. Smith remarks, survives to this day in the bridal canopy of Jewish weddings. The custom of requiring the brother to marry the widow of the deceased also appears. Undoubtedly it was of extreme antiquity. *Sadiqa* marriages were not unknown, though the reason for them was not as conspicuous as in the earlier time. Harlots had ceased to be regarded as formerly they had been. Though not yet brought under the ban of tribal statute, the changes wrought in their social status left them where they were regarded with increasing disfavour.[1] Wives or daughters who played the harlot might be burnt.[2] The great increase of " devoted women " at the numerous sanctuaries, which became in time sinks of iniquity and vice, had much to do with the decrease of harlots as individuals plying a trade of their own. Besides, if they were, as we have surmised, a relic of the old matriarchate, men would, with the progress of the centuries, lose sight of the fact and so come to regard them with less favour.[3]

[1] The Book of the Covenant in time outlawed them.
[2] Genesis xxxviii.; Dillmann, *Genesis*, vol. ii., p. 343.
[3] See Appendix II.

Authority in the home throughout this period belonged to the husband, or, if he were dead, to the
eldest son. Wives and children were under his control to a greater extent than when the clan was more
vigilant and more inclined to insist upon its ancient
rights. Even mature sons were not exempt from
paternal control. Saul goes forth obediently to look
for his father's asses, and cannot forget that he is
under authority while away; and the headstrong Absalom, lenient as David was, dares not show himself
at Court after his return from exile until he receives
royal permission. Husbands were not wanting who
deferred to their wives or gave them considerable
freedom; but no such position was accorded wives
as Professor Sayce has shown was given their wives
by the Babylonians.[1] It is improbable that the
Hebrew wife ever held property of her own or that
she engaged in business on her own account.

Children were desired, and when born, were
prized.[2] The patriarchal and other stories of the
time reveal this; and the names given even to female
babes, as " Grace " and "Pearl," suggest the delight
and high hopes of the parents. In times of sickness
in the home the father could forget his business
or the affairs of state and show a tender solicitude.
Ordinarily, where circumstances allowed of it, nurses
were employed. Games were played by the children,
and pet animals were common. The love of the
husband and father was not unconfessed. Chroniclers speak freely of it. Even the fact that a man

[1] Babylonians and Assyrians, p. 13 ff. (in *The Semitic Series*).
[2] Hastings' *Dictionary*, vol. i., p. 381 f.

was seen sporting with his wife is not hidden. The
kiss was bestowed by the father upon sons as well as
upon daughters, and courteous forms of speech were
employed that probably made it easier for adult
children to obey the behests of parents. Formal disposition of property was made at the close of life,
though the first-born was by ancient custom expected to enter upon the inheritance of the bulk of the
father's estate, as he was also expected to assume the
cares and responsibilities of the household. The
nature of the Hebrew home was such as to account
very largely for the superior character of the best
men of the time, who, on any other supposition than
that they were moulded very largely by home influence, would present to us an unsolvable enigma.

The home in which the family lived was usually the
home also of the domestic animals, built where circumstances permitted, about a court, and having its
separate chambers or apartments opening thereon,
with a chamber or chambers upon the roof.[1] The
well-to-do kept a porter or door-keeper at the single
entrance. Such a porter might serve in other and
more menial ways, as in the somewhat straitened
establishment maintained by Ishbaal, who disputed
for several years with David his father's kingly crown.
In this instance the poor woman who had charge of
the door had also to clean wheat, and, becoming weary
over her many duties, had fallen asleep, thus giving
the assassins the chance to slip in unnoticed.[2] The
couches or beds, ordinarily little more than a blanket
used upon a slightly raised platform, with which the

[1] Hastings' *Dictionary*, vol. ii., p. 431 ff.   [2] 2 Sam. iv. 4 ff.

chambers were provided, were used by day as well as by night. The siesta was universal. It was necessitated by the heat of midday, which much of the time was severe. The evening meal was the principal meal of the day ; at this guests frequently appeared. Special honour could be shown friends by sending them portions from the table. The guest if he remained overnight was still, in accordance with ancient custom, called early in the morning and sped on his way. It was a kindness to do this in a land where the wayfarer must do his journeying ere the heat of the day. As families of wealth increased in Jerusalem, and more especially in Samaria in the days of Jeroboam II., habits of luxury were formed and unblushingly indulged. The winter house in the city had its counterpart in the summer cottage among the hills, in both of which a style of living was adopted that crossed the austere principles of other prophets than Amos, the Herd of Tekoah, who was accustomed to the simplest country fare. Cedar and ivory were freely used in the construction of such houses ; and in the appointments of them, in the hangings, the rugs, the chairs, the couches, etc., a like degree of elegance was secured. Utensils of bronze, silver, and gold abounded. Wives joined their husbands and guests in their drinking-bouts and the coarse converse which formed an accompaniment of the feast. The pouring out of wine to Baal and Astarte, or even to Yahweh himself, disguised not the shamelessness of such scenes. This was the worst fruitage of the home, and this darker picture needs to be placed alongside the brighter.

As clan customs tended to pass away, the family gained in importance as a social factor in the life of the people. Becoming purer and more self-sufficing, the homes did much to keep the people from disintegration. Only on the supposition that many of these homes were the nurseries of pure sentiments and lofty ambitions, can we account for the fact that the Hebrews did not utterly succumb to the immoral practices and tendencies of the time. There may have been little moral purity at the high places; all the more reason have we for believing that the home life was in innumerable instances for the time singularly strong and pure. Like many of the Greek homes of those times the Hebrew homes encouraged industry and thrift and fostered purity; and they did so the more surely because in them the wife and mother was loved and honoured. The brave way in which Hosea struggled to make an ideal home out of the unpromising material which he put into it, gives us a glimpse by way of contrast of what a home must in those times have been where both husband and wife were sincerely striving to live up to the light vouchsafed them. Isaiah's home must have been of this character. May not thousands of the humblest of the Hebrew homes throughout these four centuries have approximated this ideal?

CHAPTER V

VILLAGE AND CITY LIFE

SOLITARY farmsteads were not to be found among the Hebrews. Like other peoples of the East, they lived in towns, in clans, septs and families, partly because such life was more convenient and more social as well as safer, and partly because it grew naturally out of their nomadic life. Among nomads the individual never thinks to set up for himself independently, but prefers, as he must, for such things are settled for him, to lose himself in his family, his sept, and his clan. Hebrew life in Canaan was, therefore, village and city life.[1] The necessity of studying the people from this point of view grows out of the nature of this life and out of the fact that these two types of life were essentially distinct, and that both had much to do in determining the character of the people.

With villages may be included, as they probably were in the thought of the Hebrews, the smaller unwalled towns, a few of which may have attained considerable size; while with cities we must include the small walled towns. The necessities of the times rendered walls the only means of defence apart from armed resistance where an enemy came upon a people.

[1] Hastings' *Dictionary*, vol. i., p. 445 ; vol. ii., p. 3 f.

They were imperatively necessary. But the circumstances of the smaller communities were usually such as to forbid their rearing walls that would afford any real defence in case of war. From wild beasts and from petty enemies, as, for example, thievish neighbours, their homes, constructed usually of stone, furnished undoubtedly considerable protection. Situated then as they were, it devolved upon the inhabitants of the villages to be watchful so that if the land was invaded by a foreign foe they might escape to the nearest walled city, to the people of whom they were closely allied, usually as fellow-clansmen. The keenly apprehensive character of these village communities frequently manifested itself. Real danger was not necessary to produce such a state of feeling; a mere rumour was enough, so insecure were they. In the days of Deborah these villages were deserted by their inhabitants, such was the activity and hostility of the northern Canaanites, who later, under Sisera, tried to bring the Hebrew clans into subjection in a campaign in which they went down ingloriously. In times of warfare, despite the precautions ordinarily taken by them, the people residing in these villages sometimes suffered severely, while those of the neighbouring city might escape. The enemy might come upon them suddenly and unexpectedly. They and their belongings might be taken possession of, and, the adult males and all sick and otherwise infirm or useless members being slain, they might be carried into captivity, the only redeeming feature of which might be that the enemy would very likely be a people somewhat akin to their own in race and manner of life. The extent to which life was thus in those times unsettled, ought not to be overlooked by the student of it.

The names for such local communities reveal little as to their peculiar character; though some things, with such clews as we have, may very reasonably be surmised. Of the several names employed the most common is bath (בַּת), *i.e.*, daughter, daughter of a city. This suggests something as to the origin of these villages, which, as already stated, might be occupied by members of the same clan as lived in the adjoining city. The relation might, however, be one of mere dependence. The village might be occupied by a conquered people or one that being weak and defenceless had been covenanted with. In an old passage in the Book of Joshua we find mention of the line of Canaanite cities that separated the tribe of Joseph from the northern clans. These, as Megiddo and Beth-shean, are named with their daughters or dependencies. Presumably most, if not all, of these daughters were unwalled villages. It is what we might expect. This way of referring to the smaller places appears in the later literature. Another word appears to have the thought of being spread out, or of openness. This reveals the unwalled character of such villages, and so has no special interest for us. Other terms appear but infrequently.

That the people of these communities were usually individual families or septs is evident; that they were also those engaged chiefly in pastoral pursuits or agriculture it is reasonable to suppose; though that there were such communities devoted largely to mining or some particular line of manufacture we cannot doubt, little as we know about such pursuits in localities which were specially adapted to them. Villages located in the little valleys among the hills where the grazing was good or the arable land fertile, may in many instances have been at considerable distance from cities of any size, but they could hardly have been far removed from each other. Regions there were where such communities were numerous, as in parts of the Shephelah. Moresheth, which once was a dependency of Gath, the home of the prophet Micah, was in the Shephelah in a region of this sort, where "there are none of the conditions or of the occasions of a large town." [1] Here there are, as G. A. Smith has shown, irregular chalk hills separated by broad glens, in which the soil is rich, with room for cornfields on either side of the perennial streams. The ruins of the region, as well as its character, attest to the fact that it was once dotted with these thrifty, enterprising communities.

But whether these villages were near each other or remotely separated, life in them was essentially country life. There was fellowship of man with man; but the country was at the door of all. They were surrounded by the sights and sounds of the country. The piping of the shepherds who closely watched their flocks on the near hill-sides, their calls across wadies to each other, and all the sounds of pastoral life could be plainly heard. The ploughman and the sower could be seen. In time of harvest all had but to step without into the adjacent fields and they could

[1] G. A. Smith, *The Twelve Prophets*, vol. i., p. 377.

bear their part; so, too, in time of vintage or when the olives must be gathered and pressed. In many of these small villages one common threshing-floor might suffice for the entire community, as might also one wine-press. Here, though families might have their individual fields for the season at least, as they surely would have their individual homes and granaries, there was something akin to a community of interests and a division of labour in the very fact that common utilities might serve one and the same community. But if the sights and sounds of country labour were thus near to all and exerted a wholesome influence, which appears at its best in men like Amos and Micah, the more potent influences of the country were also near. The pastures and cultivated fields, the sight of which was so satisfying to such a people, though they may not have had that keen sensitiveness to natural beauty which the modern man thinks he has, the lowing of cattle, the bleating of sheep, the hum of the bees, and the songs of the birds, and all the fascinating allurements of the country environ- ment, were then the lot of those who lived in these villages. Even less welcome sounds, as the roar of a lion, might occasionally be heard, though these were heard more frequently in lonelier regions. In such villages strong, healthful, independent men were bred. A large part of the population both north and south was apparently so reared. Many of these people may have had little of the culture of their city kindred; yet for this very reason they may have been purer and sturdier morally. Only on the supposition that the larger towns and the cities, which by reason

of the nature of their sanctuaries and other influences
were to a large extent pervaded by vice and disease,
were renewed from time to time, as our cities still
are, by the inflowing of the more healthy tides of life
from the country, can we account for the fact that the
collapse of the Hebrew states did not come sooner.

The walled towns and cities of the Hebrews were
usually located upon small hills. A wady on one or
more of the sides of the city was, therefore, a characteristic feature, and served for purposes of drain-
age, as it did also as a lurking-place for an enemy.
While such locations would be favourable to health,
it was not this, but the defensive nature of such sites,
which led to their being selected. The sites of most
of their larger cities were not, however, of their own
choosing. Long before their day the Canaanites had
built these, only to pass them, with the lapse of time,
over to the Hebrews. The selection of the particular
hill upon which a city should be built had been determined in part by the old roads of the land, which
ran from north to south and from the Sea of Galilee
and the Jordan to the Mediterranean sea-board.
Whether the immediate region of the site of a city
was fertile had been an altogether secondary consideration, though a site that was otherwise favourable
was considered fortunate if there was rich pasturage
and fertile fields which were not far away, for means
of transportation in those times were inefficient.
Jerusalem had more to recommend it in the way of
its inaccessibility and its practically impregnable
character ; while Samaria had a more fertile region
at its very door to which it could confidentially look

for sustenance. Judea never was densely populated,
and Jerusalem never was a great city in point of
numbers. The Northern Kingdom, on the other
hand, was capable of sustaining a large population,
as we know it did in the time of Christ, and it probably had at the time under consideration a number
of cities of considerable size.

The Hebrew cities were surrounded by walls,
which for the time served fairly well their purposes.
Assyria in her best days found some of these cities
difficult to reduce. The defensive value of the walls
was enhanced by towers in which, as well as upon
the walls in time of war, men might be placed. Careful attention was necessarily given to the care and
the guarding of the gates, of which the smaller cities
had but one, while the larger cities had several, each
of which, because it served in the main a distinctive
purpose, had its appropriate name. In some way
the military force which in time of war defended a
city was organised, for a sudden alarm was enough
to lead to a careful and systematic manning of the
walls. In the tower over the principal or only gate
was a chamber from the window of which a watch-
man could easily espy a coming runner or the ap-
proach of an enemy. The houses of these cities came
close up to the narrow streets, though they usually
had their interior court open to the sky. The life of
the family would, therefore, have been tolerably quiet,
though lived in the city, had it not been for the flat
roofs upon which the people were often to be found.
Though not as common a feature of the social life of
the people as the courts of their houses, the roofs

were largely used, and their use contributed much in the way of counteracting any tendencies to isolation which other features of their homes encouraged. The market-place within but near the gate, and a single broad way or street, served many mercantile and social purposes; but the great gathering-place was outside the principal or only gate.[1]

To the city gate men came bearing all sorts of intelligence. At one time it would be a word that would lead to the marshalling of the fighting men without the gate, that they might go forth in orderly array. To the same place they would return and would be mustered out after dividing the spoil. At another time news of some calamity was brought to the gate, the death of the King or of a son of the King, the messenger appearing with torn garment, dishevelled, and dust-covered hair. Immediately there were loud lamentations, garments were torn and faces were covered. The maidens of such a city were frequently seen near the gate. Thither, in case of the smaller cities, at least, they would come for water, their water-jars borne upon the head gracefully, and forming a pleasant contrast to the gay colours with which they were decked. Thither, the maidens also came to welcome the coming of the King or other distinguished personage, or to greet with song and dance victors of war laden with booty.

The larger cities in process of time had their aqueducts, which brought pure water from distant hills.[2] Little was done in the way of sewage dis-

[1] Hastings' *Dictionary*, vol. ii., p. 110 ff.

[2] Cheyne and Black, *Encyc. Biblica*, vol. i., c. 881 f.

posal until under the domination of the priests an
era of cleanliness if not of godliness came into vogue.
Yet there was outside the city gate the inevitable rub-
bish-pile, the city-dump, suggesting the old saying
of Yahweh, the friend of the poor : "He taketh the
needy from the city-dump and maketh him to sit
among the nobles (*i.e.,* among the liberal, the well-
circumstanced, and generous - hearted)." The famished, greedy dogs of these cities, little as they added to them æsthetically, served a useful purpose as
scavengers ; but it is to be feared that, on the whole,
city life was far from being as healthful as village
life.   It surely was not as invigorating morally.

CHAPTER VI

THE INDUSTRIAL LIFE

DURING the centuries which immediately followed their settlement in Canaan, flocks and herds had been the chief dependence of the Hebrews, for they took to agriculture but slowly. Wheat and barley, the olive and the grape, they learned to cultivate, but there is nothing to show that there was any great variety of agricultural staples. It is different during the period we are now considering. Life becomes distinctively agricultural.[1] A great variety of products appears. They still have flocks and herds, but the main dependence is upon agriculture. Wheat and barley are the great staples; the olive and the grape are even more widely cultivated; but beans, lentils, and other products are mentioned. Wine was universally used, and strong drink, made probably of the juices of other fruit than the grape, for the fortification of wine was probably unknown, was produced. Familiar among the sights of rural life was the wine-press. The possession of one was even more a mark of distinction among them than the threshing-floor with its oxen and threshing-sledge. Primitive methods of agriculture prevailed. Imple-

[1] Wellhausen, *Encyc. Brit.*, vol. xiii., p. 408; Kittel, *Hist. of the Hebrews*, vol. ii., p. 296.

ments were used, but were still of rude construction. The mention of the yoke, the plough, the ox-goad, the cart and the wagon, the harness, the harrow, the mattock, the axe, the sickle, the basket, etc., but partially suggests a type of life in which work was done very largely by hand, thus necessitating the employment of all, old and young, at certain seasons, as in the earlier time.

Small farmers there were, though the land might be in the hands of village communities or septs ; but large estates upon which scores of slaves were employed were not uncommon. The thought that the land was carefully distributed at this time among an innumerable multitude of small proprietors is foreign to fact. Those who had been able to take to themselves large holdings and utilise them had done so. Apparently, no known customs or laws interfered with their so doing. It was only with the lapse of centuries that land laws were enacted. At first the matter of tenure had been vested in the clan, in which as the population was sparse and land was abundant, there would always be a disposition to favour him who could utilise large portions. Kings had their royal estates, and princes were known as raisers of sheep and cultivators of the vine and the olive. As in Israel, so it was without, as in Moab. Like the Babylonians and Assyrians,[1] the Hebrews seem not to have thought any the less of kings and princes if they engaged in agriculture and business, especially if agents or overseers were employed. As a rule, kings might not closely look after their royal

[1] Sayce, *Babylonians and Assyrians*, p. 150.

domain, but a prince like Absalom found it easily possible to personally superintend his own farm or ranch.

The industrial life became richer and more complex in many ways during this period. There was a tendency to do more outside the home and off the estate. There were men who supported themselves by particular handicrafts. Seldom as the smith and the potter appear in ancient literature, they were in evidence, as were carpenters, masons, and workers in bronze and silver and gold. Architecture was in the main simple and plain to a degree that must have rendered the smaller towns far from picturesque, royal residences and the homes of the wealthy being exceptions to the rule. The forced labour of the King, which was not employed in constructing residences for royalty or temples, which, like that of Solomon, were little more than royal chapels, was utilised in building city walls, constructing aqueducts, and other works of public utility. That old life cannot be understood unless account is taken of the place occupied by this forced labour. The murmurs and complaints which late writers put in the mouths of the earlier Israelites may not have been altogether without warrant, for kings may have made them handle the mattock and bear burdens in their levies; but the major part of this forced labour must have been Canaanitish or foreign. Very frequently it was more to a king's advantage to spare and thus utilise a subject people or a conquered enemy than it was to put them to the sword, and consequently economic rather than humanitarian reasons carried the day.

The home was still a hive of industry. Here curds and cheese and butter as dairy products were manufactured. Here grain was parched or ground ; here flesh was both boiled and roasted. The mention of the numerous terms for kettles alone suggests a type of life beside which that of the old Saxon and Danish kings of England seems exceedingly primitive. Not so was it as regards bread and pastry making, a hole in the ground in which stones were heated being employed for this purpose. In the home cloth was woven and garments were made, the raw material as flax and wool being prepared and spun therein as in the earlier time. Cotton apparently, and linen and woollen fabrics certainly, were among the staple products of the home. The garments worn by both sexes, which differed not materially, were two, the tunic or shirt, which though usually sleeveless and short, might be worn long with sleeves, and an outer garment or robe. A tunic of ends or extremities, *i.e.*, a long tunic reaching to the ankles and wrists, was worn only by the wealthy and those of royal birth. Such, and not a garment of many colours, as even our Revisers insist on calling it, was the garment worn by Tamar, as it was also the garment given Joseph by his father. The outer garment was a more conspicuous part of one's attire. This when worn by the poor was of coarse, cheap material ; but the robes worn by the wealthy were frequently rich and costly. No part of the dress was more prized than the girdle, which might be elaborately and beautifully wrought. The present of such a girdle to a friend was considered a special mark of

favour. That the home was a place in which useful
articles were manufactured for trade is unquestionably true. It was from the home very largely that
village and city shops were supplied; though the
home with the shop or counter was often the place
of both manufacture and sale. From the home also
must have been taken many of the fabrics and utilities which were sold at the great fairs at the religious festivals.

Without the home, by pool or wady side, or near
the cistern upon which they depended for water, garments were washed. This was usually done by
pounding or treading the clothing in the water. The
verb here is suggestive; it means "to tread." The
cistern was found ordinarily in small villages and in
the country where it seemed not worth while to have
a well.[1] Even Bethlehem, which in David's day had
its well, has for centuries depended upon a cistern at
which reverent pilgrims have slaked their thirst in
the thought that they were drinking at the well of
Bethlehem.

It is just here in connection with the industrial
life that we catch sight of most of those things which
give to a country and people much which we are
wont to characterise as local colour. Some things
which we glimpse as we project ourselves in thought
back into that old time, and run to and fro in the
land, have not to do directly with the industrial life,
but most of them have. The whitewashed, dingy
buildings over which the light often plays in a fascinating way, catch our eye. The imposing walls of

[1] *Encyc. Bib.*, vol. i., c. 880 f.; Hastings' *Dic.*, vol. i., p. 444.

the larger towns and cities, with their individual gate and the inevitable watch-tower, arrest our attention, and we find ourselves wondering if the keeper will admit us or force us to remain without as suspicious-looking wayfarers. If once we get within, we are likely, we know, to be most kindly and hospitably taken in hand by some citizen who will count it a privilege to show us "the kindness of Elohim." The sights and sounds of soldierly life and warfare as we try to reproduce that old time may seem to more powerfully arrest the attention, or those associated with royalty may; but, after all, it was not the sound of the horn summoning to war the fighting men, it was the noise of children at their play that was most frequently heard. It was not the wailing of the people over the death of some prince, it was the sound of peaceful industries that broke upon the air. It was not the stoning of some reprobate, but the incoming of an ass bearing a skin of wine from a neighbouring village, or, better, a sack of wheat; not the fall of a gate-tower, but the departure of a caravan; not the devastation of a plague, but the rise of a new city: these were the things which made up the life of the people and gave to that life the larger part of its local colour.

Apart from the institution of slavery, there were strong lines of demarcation in the social life of the Hebrews. There were the beggars and other outcasts, as there were also worthless fellows who were lawless and capable of any crime then known. Then there were the rich and the poor. If the former would not be considered possessed of ample means if judged by our standards, there can be no question as to the latter. A man so poor that he must needs pawn his outer garment that he may have the wherewithal to buy the food he is to eat ere he is paid at night, when he may redeem his garment, and this, too, day after day, is poor in our eyes beyond a doubt. Yet such, wretched as they were, might rise out of their poverty. Though forced to take to the city-dump for lodgings, the needy might lift himself out of his misery. It was a long way among the Hebrews of those times from the city-dump to a seat among the nobles of the land; but Yahweh knew the way. And just here we catch a glimpse of one of the most hopeful features of that old time and life—labour was so held in honour the poor unfortunate might lift himself by industry, thrift, and integrity into a position of honour.

In speaking of the industrial life, a few words need to be said of roads and travel, though there had been little improvement here as compared with the earlier time. We read of highways or turnpikes during this period. There is no possibility of misunderstanding the word; *mesillah* (מסלה) is a raised road. The term could hardly be used of ordinary roadways; it suggests that something was done in parts of the land near the larger cities in the way of road building. The levy, or forced labour of the King, would easily render this possible.[1] Nevertheless, the roads for the most part were poor, and in many parts of the land there were no attempts at road construction. The numerous words for a path reveal that a way

[1] Num. xxi. 22 ; cf. 2 Sam. xx. 12 ff.

along which asses and mules could walk was all that most regions possessed. Bridges were seldom needed save in times of heavy rain, as even the largest streams could be forded. There can hardly have been a ferry at the Jordan, as our translators have misled us into supposing. The term may be otherwise very reasonably explained. Carts, two-wheeled vehicles, and wagons of four wheels were more frequently used during this period than earlier for conveying heavy merchandise. Asses were universally employed, she-asses being still in favour, though mules were used by the wealthy, as were horses singly or by twos and threes in chariots. The horse found favour in times of war as especially adapted to the soldiery. As the population multiplied and the peoples among whom the Hebrews lived put themselves more and more in their hands, travel appears to have increased. The traditional jealousies of the Northern and Southern Kingdoms did not keep their people from having considerable commercial and social intercourse.

CHAPTER VII

WARFARE

In the actual life of the Hebrews warfare played an important part, though the state was not organised upon a military basis, and the standing armies, that is, the seasoned soldiers who were kept from industrial pursuits or who were hired from neighbouring peoples, as was the case even in the time of David, were not large—a few thousand at the most. Kings were forced to rely chiefly upon levies from among the peasantry; and such troops made, as might naturally be supposed, sorry work of warfare, though the Hebrews, like other Semites, were not lacking in soldierly qualities. Fortunately for them the Hebrews were seldom opposed by forces more disciplined than their own before the Assyrian armies in the ninth century began to devote attention to them. We have to do then, in this chapter, with warfare not so much as an art as an occasional practice or diversion, and the effects of it as so prosecuted upon the social life. That warfare was sometimes with them a diversion, a raid being made or a campaign being undertaken with the hope of spoil, we know. Whatever may be true of progressive nations to-day, morality was among the old Hebrews largely a matter of locality.

Among the prices which they had to pay royalty for condescending to live among them was that of fighting for their houses both north and south as the caprice of a king might dictate. Rebellions in the days of David and Solomon and frequent quarrels with Philistines, Edomites, Moabites, Ammonites, and Syrians would, however, necessitate considerable in the way of stern fighting, in which, whenever the enemy got the better of them, there was often needless and brutal slaughter, for the laws of modern warfare were then unknown and the common principles of humanity unrecognised.

The bodyguard of the King, his little standing army, was always ready for action and really by its services made itself indispensable.[1] It appears to have consisted of different bodies of men, some of whom were more lightly armed than others, but all of whom were well equipped according to the best standards of military science in those days and some of whom by their great stature and strength were considered well-nigh unconquerable. In the north chariots to some extent came into use; but there could have been little use for them in the south.[2] Hilly Judea was ill adapted to them. The fighting men were quickly gathered by the sounding of trumpets or horns throughout the land. Among these, bowmen seem to have predominated, while men armed with spear and shield were to be found in large numbers. To beat their swords into plough-

[1] Cheyne and Black, *Encyc. Bib.*, vol. i., c. 312 ff. ; Kittel, *His. of the Hebrews*, vol. ii., p. 164 f.

[2] *Encyc. Bib.*, vol. i., c. 725.

shares and their spears into pruning hooks, or the opposite figure, was used so frequently by their prophets as to suggest the very general employment of these weapons. That most adults were equipped in some way, though but indifferently, for warfare, is certain. It is interesting to notice that with many the club and the sling were slow in giving way to other weapons. For a man to be unprepared and to fail to respond when the summons came would be for him to lose very largely his social standing, to say the least. Yahweh as their God had his place among them as the God of battles.

The Ark with its ephod was considered indispensable. It was borne before their armies with the cry as they took it up: "Rise, O Yahweh, and let thine enemies be scattered, and let them that hate thee flee before thee."

The men were divided into hundreds and thousands with their appropriate leaders, captains of hundreds and captains of thousands, if on their arrival by sept or clan they were not thus organised. There is little doubt that in most parts they had their local organisations corresponding to the militia of some modern nations. Many, aside from the regular forces, or bodyguard of the King, had their armour, which, however rude, would offer some protection. It is not known that the leaders were distinguished by their dress, but we know that among the Hebrews, as among the Assyrians, kings went into battle wearing their crowns and royal robes and regalia.[1] When Saul fell on Mount Gilboah he was wearing his golden crown and

[1] 1 Kings xxii. 30 ff.

anklets, and according to an improbable story they were taken to David by an Amalekite who hoped to be rewarded.[1] In battle the bowmen were specially dreaded, the arrow drawn by a strong arm being their most formidable weapon and capable of fearful execution among men but imperfectly armoured. The battle array, or line of battle, and some sort of phalanx were not unknown; but disorder in battle seems to have been the rule and could hardly have been otherwise among undisciplined troops.

If the forces of the enemy were encountered in the open field, it was considered fortunate, for otherwise it might be necessary to besiege and reduce the city into which they had fled before an end could be made to the war. Where the enemy showed an eagerness for the fray, there might be delay, while picked men or single individuals fought not in sport but in mortal combat. Such contests, though they might serve as excitants, proved sometimes brutal butcheries.[2] As they were about to join battle they raised a great cry or yell, a custom still in vogue, which has its psychological reasons as well as its extreme antiquity, which may be pled in its favour. Where the enemy retired to a walled and strongly fortified city, considerable time might elapse before he could be brought to submission, if, indeed, it were possible to reduce him. David's flight from Jerusalem was probably quite as much because he feared his capital would not be able to endure a siege as because he doubted the loyalty of some near him. Later, upon his return, his fear in the rebellion of

[1] 2 Sam. i. 10 ff.   [2] 2 Sam. ii. 14 ff.

Sheba was that Amasa by want of promptitude would allow the rebel to get north with his forces into some walled city. "Now," said the King, "shall Sheba, the son of Bichri, do us more harm than did Absalom: take thou thy lord's servants and pursue after him, lest he get him fortified cities, and escape out of our sight."[1] This difficulty which the Hebrews met in reducing forces so circumstanced would hardly be worth mentioning, so common was the experience in those days and until the invention of gunpowder and other high explosives, were it not that an advance is noticeable in strategy on the part of the Hebrews just here. Something like several months, if not a year, appears to have been spent in reducing by siege Rabbath-Ammon, the chief city of Ammon, as the name suggests. When at last Joab secured possession of the fortified water-works of the city, and perceived that the famished people could not hold out much longer, he sent to David that he might come and be on hand to receive the submission of the long-besieged city.[2] But Sheba, already referred to above, did get into the city in which his sept dwelt; and the Hebrews under the lead of Joab and his brother came upon the place and, to render the verb literally (for baskets were used then as still they are in the East), poured out a mound against the city so that it stood even with the wall and made it possible for them to put a bridge across.[3] Only by the beheading of Sheba and the casting of his head

[1] 2 Sam. xx. 6.
[2] 2 Sam. xii. 26 ff. Smith, *Samuel*, *I. C.*, p. 326 f.
[3] 2 Sam. xx. 15; Smith, *Samuel*, *I. C.*, p. 371 f.

down to the men of David did the Bichrites save themselves.

Inasmuch as little was done by the peoples whom the Hebrews encountered in warfare in the way of organising the commissariat before setting out on a campaign, the progress of an army through their country rendered it well nigh a wilderness for a decade. But in addition to the necessities of provisioning, crops were destroyed, buildings burnt or pulled down, fruit-trees felled, springs befouled or choked up, and sometimes arable land was strewn with stones. All that fiendish ingenuity could devise was at times practised. Where an army was overcome, or where a city was taken, spoil was made of everything of value, while many were carried into captivity. To an even greater extent than in the earlier period the traffic in slaves proved an incentive to such warfare. The demand was greater ; the market better. The armour of the slain went, as as among the Greeks, to the slayer. Whether the general was bound by custom to reward a soldier that captured or slew some great rebel or adversary we cannot say.[1] Undisciplined as they were in arms, the Hebrews had their rules [2] and precedents, as they had also their military proverbs. " Let not him that putteth on his armour boast himself as he that putteth it off," was one of the latter; while the appeal to antiquity furnished them with precedents, as in the case of the folly of Abimelech, the son of Jerubbaal, who was said to have lost his life at the hands of a woman who dropped the heavy rider

[1] 2 Sam. xviii. 12.   [2] 1 Sam. xxx. 24, 25.

millstone upon him as he came up under the wall of Thebez.[1]

If in any direction the men of Israel gained by warfare beyond securing for themselves for centuries national existence, it was owing to the fact that their larger wars with neighbouring peoples brought together the men of their different clans. Though their military organisations must have been largely according to clans, actual warfare threw individuals from different parts of the land together. This helped to consolidate the diverse elements of Judah more than any other one thing, unless it be their religion. So also were the various and somewhat disparate elements of Joseph united into a kingdom in which there was considerable loyalty to local institutions. The conspicuous achievements in a campaign of the men of any one city or locality would endear them to all, as the endurance of any overwhelming disaster when contending for the general good would do. There are notes in the old poetry of the Northern Kingdom that reflect this feeling. This poetry belonged to them as a people; they used it in its entirety, and were correspondingly influenced thereby.

War in those days, even more than in ours, must have brutalised men. Society was not only disorganised, it was also dehumanised by war, so needlessly bloody and cruel was it and so little disposed was the victor to allow his foe to settle back into his old ways. To the conquerors nearly as much as to the conquered certain of the baser effects of war must

[1] 2 Sam. xi. 21.

have been felt. Had it not been for the quiet and peaceful days spent in honest toil amidst the felicities of home and neighbourhood life which the Hebrews as a comparatively insignificant people among the greater world-powers enjoyed, they could hardly have wrought out for us some of the noble sentiments and lofty ideals which we find in the prophets of the closing century of our period.

CHAPTER VIII

LITERATURE AND EDUCATION

IT is extremely doubtful whether the Hebrew nomads who entered the land of Canaan in the thirteenth century B.C. were possessed of a written literature; though some of their number may have made some small use of letters. The rough life of the desert must have been unfriendly to such culture; while the life which the people lived in Egypt must have been a life out of touch with its advanced civilisation. It seems probable that the art of writing must have been learned of the Canaanites. The Tellel-Amarna tablets reveal the fact that letters were not unknown in Canaan long prior to this time. We may suppose that the folk-stories and battle-odes, of which we have remnants in the Book of Judges, were not committed to writing until some time after they were composed.[1] That there was no written literature in Israel prior to the compilation of J in the ninth century, cannot be maintained. The evidence is against such a supposition. Much of the material used by J must have long been in written form. Says W. H. Bennett: "The reader will remember

[1] Budde, *The Folk-Songs of Israel*, *The New World*, March, 1893. "In ancient times, only by a happy chance and very exceptionally were poems of this kind put into writing and transmitted to posterity."

that, before the close of the eighth century, the Israelites already possessed numerous narratives, poems, and other monuments of the revelation they had received through their national experience and their inspired teachers. During the later monarchy and the Captivity these earlier documents were combined in larger works, with various additions and other modifications."

Dr. Kittel in his *History of the Hebrews*, vol. ii., p. 95 f., is even more explicit: "The discovery of the art of writing is, beyond doubt, the most important triumph of civilisation. When and in what form this art reached Israel, we cannot say. If, as I believe, Moses was a historical personage and had been in Egypt, he would most likely have adopted the Egyptian mode of writing. But we know at the same time that there was early used in Palestine a new way of writing—the alphabetic, or, strictly speaking, consonantal script, in which the phonetic principle, already known to the Egyptians, though not carried out by them, was recognised in its immeasurable importance. This script originated as a consonantal script in Semitic soil, and was thence adopted by the Græco-Roman civilised world—with results incalculably great for it and for our civilisation. We are told that Jerubbaal-Gideon had written down for him by a young man of Succoth, casually picked up, the seventy-seven names of the aldermen and council of the town. If the statement is credible, this fact alone shows such a general spread of the art of writing as was possible only by the help of the extraordinary simplification produced in that art, in

its older form so complicated, by writing the conso-
nants alone.[1] . . . The consequence of the introduction of the new script was the beginning of
real literature. Now, the first heroic lays and the
oldest laws referred to Moses,[2] perhaps also, even
several hero stories, such as those of Jerubbaal and
Abimelech, were reduced to writing—promising beginning of a rich literature that has outlived the
centuries."

Dr. Kautzsch, in his *Literature of the Old Testament*, takes a similar position as to the compilation
of the great historical documents. He even goes so
far as to attempt to assign approximately the date of
many of the earlier pieces of Hebrew literature. "In
Israel, as in other nations, the earliest literary period
was preceded by one of song and legend. The conditions on which, in every age, the appearance of a
real literature depends—above all, the wide diffusion
of the arts of writing and *reading*, the settled life and
comparative prosperity of the people—did not exist
in Israel till near the end of the so-called age of the
Judges, certainly not during the Journey through the
Desert or whilst the tribes were incessantly strug-
gling for existence, after the immigration into Canaan."[3] He also declares : "It has been thought
necessary to date the beginnings of a real literature

---

[1] It must be said of this last statement that it lacks logical
cogency. The author's observation (vol. ii., p. 95) that the
writing on the Mesha stele proves "long previous practice in the
use of a script," is more conclusive.—Cr.

[2] "Especially Ex. xx. ff. (Decalogue and Book of the Covenant)."

[3] Page 1 of the above-named work.

not later than this period, the second half of the time
of the Judges. It must be acknowledged possible as
early as this, perhaps at sanctuaries which had long
been famous, such as those at Shiloh and Bethel,
among a hereditary priesthood of old standing, the
writing down of ancient songs or of the histories of
these sanctuaries was taken in hand. But," he adds,
"no actual proof can be adduced. It would rather
appear that we must come down to the time of David
for the writing out of the products of those earlier
days." It is interesting to notice that this scholar
names as the probable date of the Book of the Covenant in its original form, prior to 857 B.C. ; of the Saul
stories in 1 Samuel ix. ff. from 911 to 888 B.C. ; of the
David stories in 1 Samuel xvi. 14 ff.—1 Kings ii.
and the stories of David found in 2 Samuel v.–vii.
and ix.–xx. 912; the E hero stories of the Book of
Judges, from 933 to 912 ; the Blessing of Jacob (Gen.
xlix. 1–27); the Book of the Upright Ones ; the Book
of the Wars of Yahweh ; and the original form of the
Balaam discourses (Num. xxiii. f.), prior to 933.[1]
Schultz, in his *Old Testament Theology* (vol. i., p.
64), asserts : "Not only must the collection of Laws
in Exodus xxi.–xxiii. be older than the year 800 B.C.,
but a much larger part of the Pentateuch." It has
been frequently claimed of late that the higher critics hold that writing was not cultivated among the
Hebrews prior to the compilation of J. Such is not
the fact. The higher critics are quick to respond to

[1] These dates of Dr. Kautzsch are probably too early by a century. Presumably in giving them he sought to be cautious and
conservative.

the evidence of a much earlier date; though they are quite generally agreed that it is unsafe to assert that they cultivated letters prior to the time of the settlement of Canaan by these nomads.

In Part I. we took occasion to speak of the influence which individuals exerted upon the social life. We dwelt particularly upon the old vindicators or heroes who, rallying about them their own septs and clans, rid their people for the time at least of the dangers which threatened them, or eased them of the burdens they were bearing and the wrongs they were made to suffer. While admitting that these men, directly through their achievements and indirectly through the fabulous stories told of them in the old folk-lore tales, exercised a strong formative influence upon the lives of men of their time and to a considerable extent upon those of a later day, we also called attention to the fact that the leading freemen of different clans had much, perhaps more, to do in quieter ways in determining the life and character of the Hebrews. The most pervasive and most potent influences are always out of sight and are not so much those of individuals as of social aggregates or schools of thought. This is especially true of the period of the Hebrew monarchy. They had in those days their great men. David, Elijah, Amos, and Isaiah, after all reasonable deductions are made from the estimates which an uncritical age has placed upon them, are admitted to have been for their time men potent in achievement and in the influence which they exerted. Here also, as in the case of the old vindicators, there was, during the earlier centuries at least, an opportunity for the play of fancy which was not lost. The stories of the lives of such men as David, Solomon, Elijah, and Elisha were so told as to interest greatly and to stir mightily the life of those times, and, indeed, say what we will of our saner ways of getting at the facts in the lives of their heroes, these old stories still take powerful hold of us. Probably a plain statement of what Elijah, for example, did in the way of attempting to save North Israel to Yahwism would not stir us with a tithe the power that the story does when taken up in Mendelssohn's Elijah where the story as well as the music moves us.

But other influences were at work in shaping Hebrew life, and here again the work was quietly and unobtrusively done. There were literary and social movements or schools which proceeded from unknown men. Take the greater literary achievements of those centuries. The legal code known as the Book of the Covenant, and much more, it may be, which preceded the Holiness Code of a later day, represented the summation of ancient customs and of the needs of the life in which it took shape as men of sagacity understood those customs and interpreted those needs. No one individual could have done this for the Hebrews. The same is true with respect to the great narratives of their past and the chronicles of their own centuries. These were the work of social aggregates or schools in Judah and Ephraim, as critical scholars have demonstrated, though for the greater convenience we refer to the writer of J or of E. And what an influence must have been exerted by these schools and all that went before them in the way of local attempts to purify sanctuaries, to rectify customs which were injurious or antiquated and to reconstruct their past! It was the same with the prophetic movement of which we shall elsewhere speak. Though the men who belonged to the movement seemed very largely to stand by themselves, they yet represented a certain tendency of purpose and of endeavour as they were also substantially one in their achievements in literature and in life.

Here then, in the movements which reached out beyond the individual and took in a considerable number of strong men, we discover the more potent influences which shaped the social life of the people. Institutions of learning they may not have had, schools to which their boys wended their way to get the rudiments of knowledge; but somewhere these rudiments were learned by many if not by all; somehow men who served as rulers or who became useful in the great literary and civic and reform movements of their day received some training, and that, too, of a character not wholly inferior. We have to confess that of Hebrew schools during this period we know nothing. That princes were taught to read and write we know. David himself wrote the note to Joab which sealed the fate of the man who was its pitiful bearer. Jezebel wrote in the name of Ahab to the sheiks of Samaria when Naboth was to be removed. Probably education was far from universal. Those who could afford to do so may have employed private instructors for their children.[1] The real education of

---

[1] Hastings' *Dictionary*, vol. i., p. 646 f.

the home generally, aside from manual training and
the discipline it entailed, consisted in shaping mind
and heart by the frequent repetition of the old folk-
lore tales used in the earlier time and the equally
delightful imaginative literature which sprang up
so prolifically during this period.   Character shaped
under the influences of the home, reinforced by the
best oral literature the day afforded, could hardly
have come up to modern standards, but it was at
least tolerably fitted for grappling with the sterner
things of life.

Somewhere then, we must conclude, the leading
men of the day, and especially those who had to do
with the literature, were trained.   The literature itself, crude as some of it is, evidences this.   The dirge
over Saul and Jonathan and the prophecies of Isaiah
were written by men that had had some literary
training.   Even Amos, countryman that he was, with
the pleasant odor of his pastures and of his herd
clinging to him, had probably learned to write as
well as to speak forcefully his mother tongue.   The
literature of the period was not in advance of the
time in its cosmological and geographical ideas ; the
same is true of the literature as it had to do with
certain other sciences then cultivated, but it was in
some directions fairly up with it.   If it reveals dependence upon Babylonia, Phœnicia, etc., in so doing it discovers to us the fact that the Hebrews of
this age were sufficiently instructed in letters and
in some other departments of thought to be able to
absorb these ideas as they came in their way.

CHAPTER IX

MANNERS AND MORALS

Not the forms of courtesy merely but real courtesy characterised the old Hebrews. The usual greeting, put often interrogatively, "Shalom?" had to do with the health and general well-being of the one inquired after. It was followed by the same word used affirmatively. The fact that a remark or behest was courteously put appears in the particle which was employed to soften speech. This particle (נא) has sometimes the force of our "please," at other times it renders the sentence in which it appears an entreaty or a quiet, courteous command. The wish to placate or propitiate another is revealed very frequently where the speaker was the superior of the one addressed in age or social station, and is characteristic of the people who were not haughty or overbearing. Kissing even among males was no mere matter of form, as frequent prostrations were not. The latter revealed the Hebrew's conception of the dignity and worth of life quite as much as they did the kneeler's wish to stand well in the eyes of him whom he thus recognised as his superior. The Hebrew as a Semite was thoughtful rather than light and frivolous; he took things seriously, though he was not destitute of the sense of humour, as is seen in his play upon words and in other simple and innocent ways.

The genuineness of the hospitality of the Hebrews is beyond all doubt. To be inhospitable was not only to be despicable, it was also to be irreligious. Hospitality was a sacred duty. This period is even richer than the preceding period in stories of gracious hospitality. The story of Abraham's entertainment of the three strangers and that of the treatment which Elisha experienced at the hand of the Shunammite and her husband may be considered typical. The kindness shown the guest upon leaving was marked by genuine courtesy. Mere interviews could easily be terminated by a blessing upon one's undertaking, an excellent way of getting rid of a crank, or of putting an end to an interview that bade fair to be unduly prolonged. It was courteous and at the same time dignified. A discourtesy was keenly felt, and a failure to bestow hospitable treatment where it was with sufficient reason expected was considered well nigh criminal. An indignity was seldom inflicted. Where it was suffered the sufferer was loath to forget it. The treatment which David's envoys received at the Court of Hanun of Ammon, the cutting off of half their clothing and of half their beards, was considered peculiarly distressing.[1] It was in the eyes of the men of David considered a sufficient excuse for war. In actual warfare all sorts of indignities were practised quite apart from mere brutality. Nothing could exceed the shameless way in which captives of war were often led about. It is to be feared that the

[1] 2 Sam. x. 4 ff.

Hebrews in these respects vied with their neighbours. They surely did not show the foreigner the same consideration which they manifested to one of their own people, though their customs and laws inculcated kindness to strangers or aliens.[1] That there was not the bitterness which was shown in the post-exilic time is, however, indisputable. Aliens might become clients of free citizens ; while whole clans and cities might by covenant become a part of the Hebrew state. The tribe of Judah appears to have been largely constituted in this way. It was probably none the worse for it, as most of the stock incorporated was racially the equal of their own in sterling qualities.[2]

Whether manners were refined by city life may be questioned. Certainly we find no more delightful stories in which pity and kindness appear conspicuously than those of village or country life. But cities offered some advantages that the country can hardly have put within easy reach. The refining influences of such music and literature as the time afforded must have been more felt in the city than in the country. In the chief cities were gathered those men who were students of their past and wrought as present-day chroniclers. There, too, most of the bards, who still repeated the old stories or invented new ones to suit the exigencies of the hour, must have had

[1] Some of their literature reveals the contrary. The story which tells of Jacob's success in outwitting Laban may here be mentioned. —Kautzsch, *Lit. Old Test.*, p. 37.

[2] It is just here that we discover the significance of the incest story of Genesis xxxviii.

their home.   Those who went about in bands singing
and playing their instruments of music dwelt in the
cities.   If anywhere, in the cities culture was in the
very air.   So closely were these in touch with the culture of both the East and the West, that the danger
of underestimating its influence is one to which the
student of Hebrew social life is greatly exposed.

The Hebrews were an excitable people, easily
moved to wrath and as easily pleased.   The frequency
with which verbs occur expressive of tremor or agita-
tion reveals this as surely as do authentic records.
Yet such excitation did not usually go very deep
though it was sincere.   It was easily laid aside.   Sui-
cide was not discountenanced.   A man might make
way with himself and yet find a resting-place without
opposition in the tomb of his fathers.   Whether sui-
cide was common is another question and one that is
impossible to answer.   Probably save where men
were fatally wounded in battle or hopelessly pressed
by the enemy, they did not resort to self-destruction.
Life, on the whole, was satisfying and joyous.   There
was little tendency to introspection, and men were
not given to meditation.   They had their words for
anxiety and depression, but had little use for them.
Fearful they sometimes were ; but, then, life was at
times insecure.   The only wonder is that they should
have remained on the whole as joyous as they continued to be.

Old customs were cherished and old traditions
sacredly guarded.   Many usages survived for centuries.   In some places the past was, it is true, more
cherished than in others.   Certain cities had the

reputation of guarding old customs and traditions, and to these, if one wished to know the pure Israelitish usages, he must go. When, intent on capturing, dead or alive, the traitor, Sheba, the son of Bichri, Joab besieged the city into which he had fled, an old woman having a reputation for wisdom was sent forth to negotiate with him.[1] She made request that the city be spared, and pled its antiquity and the fact that it had vied with Dan as a centre of Israelitish tradition. Such places may have been few but they were significant, as they were also influential. It is likely that such cities were more common in the north than in the south. The great tribe of Joseph, which remained to the time of its fall remarkably self-sufficient and comparatively free from incorporated foreign elements, was undoubtedly conspicuous in this way. Among the Ephraimites much of the historical lore of the Hebrews was preserved; and this lore was largely used in reconstructing imaginatively their past. There was a vast amount of intellectual activity of which we know little, save what may be surmised from its fragments. But the fragments reveal love of their past and pride in their achievements. Free from the inroads which the nomads of the south made upon Judah, the proud, sturdy, self-reliant men of Ephraim retained for centuries their old manners, customs, and traditions in comparative purity.[2]

[1] 2 Sam. xx. 16 ff.; Smith, *Samuel*, *I. C.*, p. 371 f.

[2] Their hopefulness seems to have failed near the close of their career. Note the character of the E narrative. Kautzsch, *Lit. Old Test.*, pp. 44, 45. Cf. the Blessing of Moses which is late, and, though belonging to E, is fairly jubilant.

Worldly goods were prized by the Hebrews, but many were easily satisfied. They were content to live in a quiet, simple way. Only in the eighth century, and then only in the larger cities, was luxury sought and gross indulgence considered a necessity of life. The majority were content to live for the most part simply and abstemiously. They had their times of feasting and debauchery, but these occasions were limited by the circumstances and religious customs of the people. That gluttony was not unknown is evident. The occasional use of flesh, instead of the common use of it, would be favourable to excess when used. History makes it equally clear that drunkenness was frequently associated with the feasting. It became in time shockingly common at the sanctuaries, as it became a distinctive concomitant of wealth and social position. In the earlier part of our period it was not discountenanced. The story of Noah's drunkenness conveys no suggestion of censure. That women joined in such debauchery in the earlier time, as did " the wealthy kine " of Amos' day, appears from the narratives, though such conduct can hardly have been thought befitting them. After Hannah had eaten and drunk, Eli, the priest, seeing her lips move in silent prayer, said to her, " How long wilt thou be drunken? put away thy wine from thee." He supposed her to be drunk. A common name for a feast was a *mashteh* or drinking bout. One of the things to be laid to the charge of David is that he purposely, and with evil intent, made the sturdy old warrior Uriah drunk. But the offence was probably regarded lightly.

More debasing still was the prostitution which
was unblushingly practised at the great sanctuaries
under the guise of religion. Of this we shall have
occasion to speak elsewhere. It was most demoralising in its effects upon the social life of the people.
That there was an element which appears still earlier
living very near the line of criminality from which
the criminal classes were recruited is not to be overlooked. It was made up of men and women who
were known as "worthless." Sons and daughters of
Belial they were called ; and worthless they were if
they are to be judged from their shamelessness.
Utterly wanting in veracity and integrity, they were
willing to sell themselves cheaply in almost any
market. There were also those who went about as
slanderers. The very verb which commonly means
to go about (רגל) gave the Hebrews the name by
which these individuals were known. It is very
likely that the drunkenness and lewdness of many of
the sanctuaries led to the multiplication of the latter
classes.

Anything in the nature of an abstract ideal must
have been far from the thought of the Hebrews ; yet
that they possessed unconsciously an ideal we can
see from a study of the Book of the Covenant, which
we shall take occasion to examine carefully in our
next chapter. This code reveals the fact that injury
of one's Hebrew neighbour was not tolerated, and
that unkindness to aliens and dependents was discouraged. Violence in the home was allowed to an
extent that to us seems revolting, but there were
limits here beyond which one could not go with im-

punity. The reviling of Yahweh, of the King, or of one's parents, was not allowed, while untruthful speech and false witnessing were punished. Altruistic sentiments were not largely demanded by this code, though they received some recognition, while in actual practice altruism had necessarily considerable place. There was little effort on the part of the Book of the Covenant to cultivate mere sentiment in any direction; it deals chiefly in prohibitions. One might live up to the letter of the law and yet be selfish and base at heart.[1] But if the ideal thus presented required little in the way of real heart-culture, it nevertheless expected considerable in the way of actual conduct. Men who were good at heart probably found little wanting in this code; its imperfections could not have been felt much before the days of the greater prophets. Even then the changes wrought in it were largely in the way of multiplying its concrete prohibitions.

[1] Still the fact that this code was largely supplementary of the old clan and city customs, regulations, and laws, keeps us from speaking too confidently of their ideals further than to say that they had to do largely with externals.

CHAPTER X

LAWS AND THEIR INFRINGEMENT

LAW as law was unknown in early Israel. The Hebrew clans had their customs, and the conduct of individual members of these clans was determined by, or in case of violation, judged in accordance with, these customs, the freemen of the clan being the judges. Penalty was as much a matter of custom as was conduct. The judges could not impose arbitrary or unreasonable punishments without endangering the very life of their clan. When, however, custom failed in a specific case, judgment could be rendered and new precedents might be made which in process of time would crystallise into customs. To such an extent was life under the domination of the clan in the time of the vindicators that we hear little of legal matters. It is possible, with a good degree of plausibility, to surmise how individual offenders were dealt with, but we have few specific cases. When we come down to the time of the monarchy we discover a difference when the King as civil head and chief-justice appears; but we have already seen that clan life and clan customs long survived alongside the monarchy. The freemen of septs and of clans, and especially the freemen of cities, had matters of law, so far at least as local affairs were concerned, in their

177

hands. The ancient and fundamental law of the land, we must conclude, originated in the various clans. What this law was we shall have occasion to notice later; it now behooves us to look more closely at other sources or fountains of law than the clan, for these other sources came into greater prominence as the clan organisation decreased in importance, as it did in the days of the monarchy.

To just what extent kings contributed to the making of law among the Hebrews cannot be accurately determined, yet we can discover by patient research several directions in which they must have made themselves powerfully felt. That they could place a taboo in times of war upon certain things, as food or the spoil of the enemy, is evident from the fact that Saul, the last of the old vindicators, was able to do this. The violation of such a taboo meant death to the violator, unless, indeed, as could rarely have happened, the people insisted that a substitute be found. In this instance, though actuated very likely by worthy motives, Saul made a questionable use of his prerogative, for abstinence from food and drink caused the people to faint ere nightfall and so kept them from pressing the flying foe, as it also led to such a lack of restraint after sunset when they fell upon the spoil of the enemy as brought confusion upon them. Ordinarily such a taboo might have proved advantageous, as when making the sack of a town; for such a taboo might extend so far as to cover the slaughter of the innocent and the violation of women. It is to be noticed that Saul, in declaring the taboo, said: " Cursed be the man that eateth

any food until evening." It was thus that a taboo
was declared by a leader or king, and the fact that a
curse hung over them, the violation of which was an
awful offence against Yahweh, that was to be followed
by death, effectually restrained the people. Such a
curse might be made to hang over those who attempted to rebuild a city or to do anything which
might militate against the common good. In case a
city failed to respond to the call of a general or king
in time of war, a curse might be pronounced against
the city. This power to curse would have a tendency
to effectually restrain cities from refusing coöpera-
tion, whatever the effects might be upon those immediately concerned. On the other hand, the cursing
of an enemy might greatly hearten the forces of
Israel when going out to battle. The extent to which
a ruler might make use of his power just here is seen
in the writings of the Deuteronomist, where a curse
is pronounced upon the makers of graven or molten
images, upon him who treats lightly and disrespect-
fully his parents, upon him who removes his neighbour's landmark, upon him who leadeth astray the
blind, upon him who perverteth the judgment of the
stranger, the fatherless, and the widow, upon him
who committeth fornication with man or beast, upon
him who secretly smiteth his neighbour, etc.[1] So also
we may see from the Deuteronomist the extent to
which an individual might in the thought of the time
be blasted by a curse. It might be made to follow
him into all the ramifications of his life, social and industrial. Here the Deuteronomist, though subse-

[1] Deut. xxvii. 15–26.

quent to the period we are considering, may be taken as revealing how much power a king might have in this direction. It was probably thus rather than by mere civil enactments and decrees that some kings made themselves felt as fountains of law and authority. The putting of a city under the ban so that all save such imperishable things, as silver and gold, must be destroyed may here be mentioned as determining the conduct of those warring against a city. Individual compunctions and preferences were then laid aside, even individual greed had then to be restrained. It is probable that such devotement of cities belongs to the later time rather than to the earlier, to the time of priestly domination after the Exile rather than to the days of the kings or the vindicators; but that it was sometimes employed by both kings and vindicators we know.

In other and more important ways the King might make himself felt as a lawgiver. He might give specific charges relative to the treatment of individuals or to the conduct of a campaign or the siege of a city that would have only local significance; but he might also make decrees that would long have power in civil as also in ecclesiastical affairs, for in religion he was preëminent. He was recognised as priest and often performed priestly functions; but he also had power of determination in matters of ritual, in the location of sanctuaries, in the appointment of priests, etc. Isaiah may have had unworthy kings in mind when he pronounced a woe against those who decree unrighteous decrees, as the writer of Proverbs must have reflected the conditions which held in the older, as well as in his own time, when he spoke of kings as those who reign, and of princes as those who decree justice. The King might sit in the gate or in judgment hall and give judgments in cases brought to him where the fear of the miscarriage of justice in lower tribunals or their incompetence to deal with the cases led men to look to him. In so doing the King might make precedents that would have binding force for generations. As the fountain of justice and the supreme tribunal the King must have had much to do in shaping the laws of the land.[1] To be derelict here, as we see in the case of David, was for a king to imperil his throne, if not his royal house. The King might fix the tribute of a subject people, as he might also determine the amount and nature of a tax to be levied at home. The extortion of Solomon in this direction prepared the way for the rebellion of the northern clans in the days of his son. Kings might also make foreign treaties and determine foreign relations, and so become in a small way fountains of commercial and international law. Finally we may notice that whatever may have been the functions of the freemen of clans and of cities in civil affairs, there can be no doubt that kings could set in motion these bodies of freemen and so influence legislation in so far as it belonged to them to legislate.

The ministers of even the greater sanctuaries could have done little in the way of giving shape to the laws of their time. The priestly legislation belonged

[1] Kittel, *His. of the Hebrews*, vol. ii., p. 301; Hastings' *Dictionary*, vol. ii., p. 842.

to the Jews of a later day, the time of and subsequent to the Exile. In the days preceding Josiah the priests were without organisation. The different sanctuaries were practically independent of one another, and often apparently in rivalry with one another. As ministers of local sanctuaries these men were not beyond serving the King in humble ways quite apart from their ordinary vocation. Sons of priests, men in years and themselves ministers of local shrines or sanctuaries, were not above service as spies or go-betweens in David's day; and one of these, as we know, upon a certain occasion served as a messenger, pitting himself in so doing against a negro. Indeed, this man, Ahimaaz by name, seems to have had an enviable reputation as a long-distance runner.[1]

Men of Yahweh, known to the time subsequent to David as prophets, by their oracular announcements determined in some measure the laws under which the people were to live, because they were supposed to sustain a peculiar relation to Yahweh. This may have had something, though not as much as a misunderstanding as to the place of the priest in the legislation, to do in fixing in the minds of later generations the thought that the laws of the Hebrews were the direct and unequivocal decrees of Yahweh himself, when the real facts were quite the contrary. Laws originated among the Hebrews as among other peoples of antiquity.[2] If in any respects their laws were superior, if there were directions in which there

[1] 2 Sam. xviii. 27.
[2] W. Robertson Smith, *O. T. in the Jewish Church*, p. 339 ff.

were marks of a loftier ethical character, we must seek for the causes thereof in the character of the people themselves and in the nature of their conceptions of Yahweh.

When we come to the laws themselves we are interested to find that the period of the monarchy produced the first formal legal code, the Book of the Covenant,[1] as it was called. This codification belongs, probably, to the eighth century. It cannot have been earlier, though some of its provisions undoubtedly had their roots in the old clan life of the people. It is not merely the fact that the laws are mostly those of an agricultural people, for Hebrew life was largely agricultural to the end, nor is it that there are other marks of a primitive character; it is rather the strong individualism of the code that guides us in determining its date. Men are dealt with as men, rather than as but partially responsible members of clans. It is the individual who is addressed in the prohibitions as it is the individual against whom the threatenings are directed. To this law-book we must go for laws of the time, if not for the earlier and previously uncodified laws, while for a conception of the penalties that followed upon the infringement of these laws we may study particular cases as they come up in the history of the period, as we may also go, as we are bound to do, to the code itself. The one study must supplement the other.

Among the Hebrews a considerable number of

[1] *O. T. in Jewish Church*, p. 333 ff.; Kautzsch, *Lit. O. T.*, pp. 7 f., 29 ff.; Budde, *Rel. of Is. to Ex.*, p. 31 ff.

offences were capital offences. In some cases death was inevitable, no circumstances could arise that would make it possible to set free the offender ; in other cases extenuating circumstances were allowed to intervene, and might lead to a money payment being accepted, or possibly to an acquittal. The blaspheming of Yahweh was punishable by death. There is a distinct prohibition against blaspheming God (Ex. xxii. 28). The verb (קלל) means to make light of or revile, rather than curse or curse in the name of. This is to be studied in connection with the third of the Ten Words : " Thou shalt not bear (נשא) falsely (or to a falsehood) the name of Yahweh, thy Elohim." This prohibition was against swearing falsely in the name of Yahweh,[1] and not against blasphemy. We have put the first-named prohibition in place of the second, and that even we have misunderstood, though not without happy effects upon our moral life. Oaths, or swearing in the name of God, a common habit that is justly thought reprehensible to-day, was not uncommon among the Hebrews. It seems not to have been condemned. Witness the oath with which upon occasion Joab addressed David as typical.[2] In the case of Naboth, who was unjustly accused of blasphemy, the penalty inflicted for the supposed offence by the free citizens of his city was death. The word for to curse (ברך), used in the charge brought against him, is unusual in

[1] Or Elohim. The Book of the Covenant was probably of Ephraimite origin, as also was the Decalogue. Hence the frequent use of Elohim.
[2] 2 Sam. xix. 7.

the sense in which it is here employed; but there is no doubt as to the nature of the charge.

The blaspheming of the King was also punishable by death. This was true of the ruler whoever he might be or whatsoever the name by which he might be known. The term used in the prohibition (Ex. xxii. 28) is "the exalted one" (נשׂיא). Joab expected Shimei to be put to death because he had blasphemed David, Yahweh's anointed. A part of Naboth's alleged offence was that he had blasphemed the King, Ahab. The story of the punishment of Miriam, who expostulated with Moses, according to the Ephraimite narrative, because he had married a negress, or Cushite,[1] should not be overlooked. Moses was the civil head of the people in the thought of the narrator. So, too, the blaspheming of one's parents was punishable by death. This prohibition (Ex. xxi. 17) should be compared with the fifth of the Ten Words, the command to honour father and mother. The smiting of one's parents came in the same category as the blaspheming of them.

A sorceress, one skilled in magic (מכשׁף), must be put to death. This, very likely, was a late requirement. It accords with Deuteronomy (xviii. 10). It is not out of harmony with the story of the witch of Endor, which, as we have it, may be late. During the greater part of our period divination and sorcery must have been practised without let or hindrance. The same may be said of the prohibition of the worship of

---

[1] The probability that the Cushites were not of negro blood is asserted by some of our leading Old Testament students.—Cheyne and Black, *Encyc. Bib.*, vol. i., c. 967 f.

other gods, the infringement of which, was to be followed by the death - penalty.   Fornication with a beast brought upon the guilty party, if detected, death.   The stealing of a Hebrew and the selling of him into slavery, an offence, it is to be feared, that was exceedingly common in some parts of the land, was a capital crime.   Manslaughter was punishable by death.   There is a distinct statement that may be compared with the sixth of the Ten Words.   A premeditated attempt to slay a neighbour was to receive the death-penalty.   Where men contended with one another and one injured the other with fist or stone, he must make amends by a money payment for the time lost.   Presumably if the injury resulted in death, he must suffer death.   If in such contention a woman with child was injured, a fine was to be imposed.   In case death ensued, the penalty was to be death.   In all cases of injury of man by man the recompense was to be according to the injury inflicted : eye for eye, tooth for tooth, etc., with the privilege of money payment where the injured party could be induced to consent to such reparation.

Specific fines were imposed in cases of theft, as five steers for a steer, four sheep for a sheep.   He who killed a thief in the act of thieving at night was acquitted ; but he who killed one by day must make some recompense.   Where property left in the hands of another was stolen or lost, it was to be made good. Borrowers were to make good the property borrowed if lost or injured.   This law probably accounts for the painful exclamation of the poor man who lost the axe in the water: "Alas, master! for it was borrowed." Too poor to own an axe, he was too poor to pay for a borrowed one that he had lost. The story of the miracle reveals this as it does also the fact that the prophets of those times were minutely interested in the social well-being of the people. A man setting a fire was responsible for any loss it might occasion if it spread into a neighbour's field. In questions of dispute over trespass or over lost beasts or merchandise, the litigants were to appear before God at the local sanctuary, where, in some way, apparently by lot, the case was to be decided, and the one declared guilty was to double to his neighbour his loss. We have here, perhaps, something akin to the old ordeal by fire or water in which the securing of justice was a very precarious matter. Where money was loaned to a fellow-Hebrew, interest was not to be exacted. This statute, it is to be feared, was frequently violated. The fact that no penalty was affixed may partly account for its violation. Where garments were taken in pledge, they were to be returned at nightfall. A stranger must not be oppressed. The sacred laws of hospitality were to hold.

The seventh of the Ten Words prohibits adultery. The code provides that in case a virgin was enticed, marriage was to follow and the usual dowry was to be paid the father of the girl, unless he forbade marriage, in which case the dowry was still to be paid, according to the dowry of virgins at the time, that is, virtually according to their price. The fixing of a definite sum, 50 shekels, in Deuteronomy belonged to a later day.

The laws in regard to veracity deserve consideration. The malicious circulating of a false report was forbidden, likewise the leaguing of one's self with an unrighteous witness. All forms of misleading the people and of the wresting of judgment were included. The poor were not to have justice denied them, and judges were not to receive gifts.

There were laws which had to do with concubinage and slavery. A Hebrew woman might, under circumstances not uncommon in those times, become the handmaid, that is, the slave of a Hebrew, as where a father, perhaps because of poverty, elected to sell his daughter. A slave thus acquired was usually supposed to become the concubine of her master; at all events she might be made a concubine and rear children to him; but if the master were not pleased to retain her in this relation, he was to allow her to be redeemed. He could not sell her to a foreign people. Apparently he might, if she were not redeemed, sell her at home.[1] He might give her to his son to wife. In this case he was to treat her as a daughter rather than as the concubine of his son. Even in case he kept her for himself he was not to curtail her food and clothing. The mention of these suggests the interesting fact that, as in the old nomadic time each wife had her tent, so later, when settled, the Hebrew husband either put a separate establishment at the disposal of each wife, or gave each, as was probably more customary, separate apartments in his own house.

A Hebrew man might be bought as a slave, but

[1] Under certain circumstances she was to be set free.

after six years of servitude he was entitled to freedom. If married when he entered the man's service, his wife and children were to be freed with him. If, on the other hand, he chanced to have a wife which his master had given him, he must, though the wife may have borne him children, go out alone. The wife and children were the master's. Where the slave was attached to his family and his master, and preferred to remain in servitude, he might become a bondman for life; but not until he had been taken to a local sanctuary and had had his ear pierced with an awl by the minister, not so much to mark him as a bondman as to symbolise his perpetual, voluntary devotement of himself to his master. Ordinary slaves, especially those other than Hebrew, have little attention given them in the early legislation that has come down to us. That such a slave might be beaten or otherwise severely dealt with, if the master did not kill him outright, is evident. In the sight of the law he had but injured his own property; yet if the master put out an eye or knocked out a tooth he must free his servant. In case he killed his slave he was to be punished; how, we do not know. Probably some fine was imposed by clan or city.

A man was held responsible for any injury which a beast of his might do. If a bull or steer killed a man, the beast alone must be killed; unless, indeed, the owner was aware beforehand that it was a dangerous animal, in which case the owner and beast must both die; though there might be here, as was probably the case earlier of all deaths by

violence, a blood-wite, according to the station of
the individual killed. In the case of a slave being
so killed, a fixed fine of 30 shekels was imposed.
Where the beast of another fell into a pit carelessly
left open and was killed, the owner received full compensation on the ground of criminal neglect. Similarly, if one man's beast killed another man's beast,
there must be recompense. Where a vineyard or
field was injured by a neighbour's beast, the owner
must make restitution. A stray beast, if found,
must be returned to its owner. Where an ass had
sunk under its load, its owner, if one chanced upon
him, must be helped.[1]

Other laws of the Book of the Covenant were of a
ritualistic character. The law concerning the first-
born of man was certainly, and that concerning the
first-born of beasts and the first-fruits was, in all
probability, much older than the code of which it
formed a part. According to this law these belonged
to God, but the first-born of man and beast might be
redeemed. We have a reflection of this law in the
story of the attempt to offer Isaac, and in the stories
of the devotion of Samson and Samuel, the first as a
Nazarite, the second as an attendant at the sanctuary
of Shiloh. The hebdomadal division of time appears
in the requirement of a weekly day of rest. Whether
the provision for a seventh year of rest belongs to the

[1] The incomplete character of the Book of the Covenant as a
codification of the laws of the Hebrews of the time is seen if we
stop to reflect that it is silent upon many important matters, as, for
example, the holding and conveyance of real estate, the status of
free citizens, etc.

Deuteronomist we cannot say positively. It looks like some of his well-known legislation, much of which was of an impracticable character. The law in regard to feasts has certainly been worked over by the Deuteronomist. It is in his style and agrees substantially with his requirements. So far as we are able to determine from the actual records of the time, but one great annual feast was observed during the period. The Book of the Covenant prescribes an altar of earth; though it permits the use of one built of unhewn stones. The early altars, which we encounter in the literature, were great stones. The only reference to earth being used for the purpose in actual history is in the story of Naaman, who begs for two mules' burden of earth, that he may worship Yahweh on his own soil. This did not forbid the erection of a stone altar upon this earth. Offerings were to be of two kinds, burnt offerings and peace offerings, which appear to have been apart from the regular and invariable offering of the blood and the fat. This accords with the chronicles of those times. The prohibition of torn flesh as food was in agreement with ancient Semitic thought. It is not that the torn flesh is holy, for it is to be cast to the dogs. It is because they who eat flesh are Yahweh's people, and because only flesh of beasts which have been properly bled in the killing, can be eaten. Unless the blood has been poured out and the fat has been burnt, it is unfit for food. The prohibition of image-making and idolatry was certainly late, though not necessarily as late as the Deuteronomist, for we find in the prophets of the eighth century the strongest condemnation of all worship of other gods and of all forms of image-worship. The prohibition against covetousness, on the other hand, is very likely much later than the Deuteronomist. It is certainly too abstract a conception to have had a place in the original of such a concrete law-book as the Book of the Covenant.

In capital offences death was by stoning. Condemned men were taken outside the village or city and stoned by men delegated to do so. Where the crime was murder or manslaughter the immediate friends of the dead were allowed to take part in the execution. Naboth was put to death by stoning as one who had committed a capital offence. "Then they carried him forth out of the city, and stoned him with stones, that he died." Tamar, who had played the harlot, according to a story of the time, barely escaped death by stoning. In real life her chances of escape would have been small. In a story of a later day a man who had broken the Sabbath during the wanderings in the wilderness was stoned to death. Even where enraged people took the law into their own hands, this was the method of lynching. Thus did David come near ending his life at the hands of his men, when he left his encampment at Ziklag unguarded, and the Amalekites spoiled it and carried off all the women and children, together with all the personal property. So, also, according to the E narrative, the two spies, Joshua and Caleb, narrowly escaped being made way with. Throughout the period capital offences when left to the freemen of clan or city were atoned for in this barbarous fashion; but when kings wished to make way with those whom they adjudged worthy of death, they despatched them quickly by some member of their bodyguard, to whom the office of executioner was probably assigned. The violators of covenants, which, being mutual agreements, were looked upon as possessed of legal character, were differently disposed of because of the covenant oath, the breaking of which was an offence against Yahweh, the God of the covenant. As we see in the story of Rizpah,[1] according to which two sons and five grandsons of Saul were put to death by the Gibeonites, covenant breakers were slain and exposed before Yahweh, who may here have been identified with the sun. The bodies of these seven men were left suspended, until the flesh had dried away from their bones, upon the side of a great cliff or rock, upon which, because of its supposed sacred character, they had been sacrificed to Yahweh. Rizpah's sacred, self-imposed duty was to remain upon the top of the rock and keep away by night and by day, birds and beasts of prey from the exposed bodies that in due time what remained might be buried.

In capital offences men were not condemned without two or more witnesses, and inasmuch as the freemen of clans or of cities were the judges, the condemnation and execution of an innocent man must have been of rare occurrence. Only when a ruler like Ahab was determined the supposed of-

[1] 2 Sam. xxi. 1 ff.; Smith, *Samuel*, *I. C.*, p. 374 ff. Cf. Num. xxv. 4.

fender should suffer could worthless men be put forward as witnesses with any reasonable hope of securing condemnation, unless the party against whom the charge was lodged was guilty. The guilt of Naboth's death belonged quite as much to his judges, who knew the character of the witnesses brought before them and the reputation of Naboth himself for probity, as to Ahab and Jezebel.

The various sanctuaries and altars of the land were places of asylum whither the criminal, real or supposed, might flee for refuge. Adonijah took refuge in the House of Yahweh in Jerusalem after his attempt to seize the throne had been foiled. The lateness of the story accounts for some of its features as it now stands, but in the main it is characteristic of the time. Any sanctuary of the land might be so used; as Dr. Bacon says: "The right of asylum was originally connected in Israel, as among other ancient peoples, with sanctuary and altar."[1] We, therefore, are not surprised that we find no trace of cities of refuge in the indubitable historical documents of the time. Of jails or prisons there could have been few, for most serious offences were capital offences. Men who were really guilty were put to death, and that, too, with the same despatch with which they buried a corpse, instead of being incarcerated. Kings appear to have had prisons, or houses of guard; but they were probably ordinary buildings devoted temporarily to the purpose. Toward the close of the period something in the nature of dungeons or pits used as places of confinement is

[1] *Triple Tradition of the Exodus*, p. 117, note.

mentioned. Such must have been at the best vile places. Similarly in villages and cities such houses or pits might upon occasion be temporarily used as houses of detention ; but the chief dependence must necessarily have been the men left to guard the prisoners.

On the whole, we are forced to conclude that justice was more secure among the Hebrews of this period than in England in the days of King John or even in the time of Elizabeth. Here, as in many other directions, the civilisation of the Hebrews, imperfect as it must have been, was superior in many respects to that of England in the tenth and even in the twelfth century of our Christian era. The indebtedness of Europe to Semitic Asia has been great ; but the slowness with which the ancient West availed itself of the superior civilisation of the ancient East is matter for wonder though easily explainable.

CHAPTER XI

THE land upon which the Hebrews lived had its convulsions of nature as it also had its catastrophes and afflictions of a milder sort. Most of these indirectly, if not directly, entailed loss of life. Destructive earthquakes, however, were infrequent, yet seismic convulsions were known to have occurred at long intervals which brought death to the inhabitants and caused great damage to property.[1] An earthquake of sufficient destructiveness to give its name to an age, so that it formed a point of departure in fixing the date of an incident, as was the case in Amos' day, should here be mentioned. He tells us he had his visions "two years before the earthquake." This same convulsion of nature appears to have been alluded to by other prophets. It occurred in the reign of Uzziah and made a great impression upon the generation to which Amos belonged, and was apparently remembered long afterward. Farther on in his prophesies Amos, it is thought, alludes to it when he says: "I have overthrown some among you, as when God overthrew Sodom and Gomorrah, and ye were as a brand plucked out of the burning." A leading biblical scholar is probably not far out of the way in

[1] Hastings' *Dictionary*, vol. i., p. 634.

thinking he can discover in the third division of this prophet's book, "A constant sense of instability, of the liftableness and breakableness of the very ground of life."[1] Surely such an affliction would at the least furnish a man with Amos' sensitiveness to nature the basal part of his imagery as a prophet of doom. The common name for an earthquake, "a shake," is of such a character as to render it difficult to decide always when a writer had the more violent phenomena of nature in mind ; but that some do refer to these in using the term is extremely probable in certain instances and indubitable in others. Still it is not the frequency of these earthquakes and the loss entailed by them that are to be noticed so much as the effects upon life in the way of unsettling it.

Other calamities, as famine and pestilence, were more frequent and were vastly more destructive of life. Locusts and caterpillars, blasting and mildew, when prevalent may not have destroyed crops to so great an extent as to lead to prolonged or widespread want, but there were seasons of drought so continuous at times that famine inevitably followed. When this happened, many of the poorer classes were carried off, forced as they were ordinarily to live upon the verge of starvation in their struggle for the means of subsistence. No affliction is more frequently mentioned. That the J and E narratives in Genesis both speak of famine is significant. These things are not talked about if they do not occur. There was, we read, a famine in the days of David. While questioning the statement, which at best represented the

[1] G. A. Smith, *The Twelve Prophets*, vol. i., p. 68.

ordinary opinion as to its cause, in this instance, we yet conclude that then and at other times the land was probably so afflicted. Inasmuch as such calamities never seemed far away to the mass of the people who lived in constant dread of them, they should not be overlooked by the student of their social life. By producing a sense of uncertainty and insecurity, and by leading men to conclude that their God was unkindly disposed, they unsettled life to an alarming extent.

Even worse in their destructiveness and in their effects upon society were the awful plagues which in those times devastated the East. The maritime regions and the lowlands must always have suffered more than the comparatively salubrious highlands where the Hebrews dwelt; yet such was the nature of some of these plagues that they must have often reached the hill-folk. In our endeavour to understand these afflictions we get little help in an etymological way. The Hebrew terms used convey generally the thought of smiting, thus leaving us after a careful study of them very much in doubt as to their peculiar character. There is, however, one term that has, not without reason, been thought to refer to the bubonic plague that should be specially noticed. The word *swellings* (עפלים) occurs in 1 Samuel v. 6 ff., and in Deut. xxviii. 27. It is probable that the story of the capture of the Ark by the Philistines, the plague its retention brought upon them and the measures devised for its return, belongs to the old Ephraimite narrative of the seventh century; though it is not unreasonable to suppose that there may have been some traditional basis for the story. There is nothing intrinsically improbable in the thought that the Philistines may at some time have taken the Ark of Yahweh, or that, if a pestilence came upon them while they had the Ark in their hands, they, as well as the Hebrews, would naturally connect the two in thought. What, however, we are specially concerned to notice is that the writers of E and the Deuteronomist, not far from the close of our period, were conversant with a plague, which, as described by them, answers to the fatal bubonic plague. As H. P. Smith says : " We can hardly go astray in seeing a description of the bubonic plague." [1] And just here we may notice the fact that the people of the East have long known that rodents carry this plague may have to do with the introduction of the rodents, mice or more probably rats, in the narrative, and the story of the offering of the images of them in gold.[2] They propitiated Yahweh by an offering of five images of the swellings and of five images of the known disseminators of the plague. The fact of redactional changes in, or of additions to, the text here means simply that writers later than E knew more of the special kind of plague described and of its causes than he did. This may be true of each redactional note, even the late mention of " ships " in the Septuagint, because it is by means of ships that wharf-rats find their way from country to country.

[1] H. P. Smith, *Samuel, I. C.*, p. 40.
[2] Ibid., p. 43 ; cf. here Hitzig and Wellhausen. See also Crookshank, *Bacteriology and Infective Diseases*, 4th ed., 1896, p. 252 ; E. H. Hankin, *Ann. de l'Inst. Pasteur*, vol. xiii., p. 387.

Afflictions of this nature, even where they did not reach the hill-folk to any extent, would greatly unsettle life, loosening the very bonds of society. More even than now would they do so; and in these days a plague is greatly dreaded in the Orient by those interested in social betterment. Sometimes there would be greater dismay because the high places at which the people worshipped proved breeding-places and centres for the dissemination of the most destructive diseases and plagues. To feel that their God was showing himself to be treacherous, that just in proportion as they remembered him they were brought to confusion, would prove peculiarly perplexing and unsettling in its effects upon life. With their " devoted women " and their fearful excesses these high places were so shameful that we would fain hesitate to speak of them. We can only throw out the suggestion that here life was morally contaminated, as it was also to a considerable extent unsettled socially.

Of the various forms of sickness and disease with which individuals were afflicted we cannot speak at any length, for nothing like a careful study of symptoms was then made among the Hebrews, and naught save the rudest efforts at classification attempted. Occasionally we get a hint that enables us, with a good degree of plausibility, to surmise what the sickness afflicting some individual was. We read of Ahijah, the keeper of the sanctuary at Shiloh, that his eyes were set or fixed by reason of age. There is a similar statement concerning an earlier keeper of the same sanctuary; but this is rejected as a gloss by textual critics. We may not unreasonably speak of this particular malady as cataract; this leaves the eyes fixed or set. For such an affliction, even in its earlier stages, they could have had no remedy. We may think of the son of the Shunammite as being prostrated by the heat. The boy went out with his father among the reapers only to fall later as the heat increased with the cry, "My head; my head!" Soon after, he died.[1] So terrific was the heat often at midday as to force men engaged in battle to desist. Where men kept up violent exercise they must frequently have suffered from prostration. Fevers were common, and for them they had their term expressive of heat or burning. In a petulant fit David, exasperated against Joab because of his perfidy, names the catalogue of diseases and other maladies which he would have come upon his kinsman and his house. Among these he names leprosy and an issue, the latter probably an unnamable disease growing out of gross sexual indulgence. It may, however, have been a case of bleeding piles. Nabal's death was in the nature of apoplexy. Insanity seems not to have been uncommon. Saul was afflicted with melancholia. David saved himself upon occasion by impersonating a madman as one perfectly conversant with demented persons; while Achish of Gath revealed by his remark, which presumably was not humorous, that all too many of his own people were similarly smitten.

Among the Hebrews there was the suffering caused by protracted sieges, when the people of these cities were reduced to the point of devour-

[1] 2 Kings iv. 18 ff.

ing such animals as the wretched dogs which in-
fested them as scavengers, and even their own off-
spring. These were things that bestialised life and
took out of it, with sad frequency, its finer strands.
We almost wonder that society in those days had
recuperative power enough to rally from the effects
of its grosser and more demoralising indulgences
and afflictions.

The sparseness of the population throughout the
land accounts for the prevalence of wild beasts. That
they were common in those days as they are in India
to-day, and that death was not infrequently to be
charged to a lion, a bear, a wolf, or a serpent, we
know. Few regions were rid of these pests. The
fear of them was well nigh universal. To protect
the flock from the lion and the bear was part of the
duty of the shepherd. The appropriate epitaph of
many might have been the well-worn phrase, "a lion
met him in the way." Perhaps the best thing said
of any one of David's big fighting men, and he had
thirty or more who specially distinguished themselves, was that concerning Benaiah ben Jehoiada,
who was wont to track lions through the snow to
their lairs and slay them.[1]

Here again we are interested to note the social
effects of the maladies with which men were afflicted.
The people of those times were not without doctors,
for we read of the *rôph^e'îm*, or healers, as they were
called ; but it is unlikely that these men were skilled
or that they were familiar with any remedies which
were not generally known to housewives. They

[1] 2 Sam. xxiii. 20.

were little better than the medicine man among our American Indians. It is probable that they were not always called in when within reach. In case of sickness it seems to have been quite generally customary to leave the unfortunate one to suffer while the head of the family hied him to some sanctuary of repute with an offering and the query whether the sick should recover. The keeper of the shrine would determine by sacred lot, and if a negative reply were given, what folly to attempt to do anything for the patient. If he had not died he must die, for it was so determined. If he were certain to recover there was no occasion for anxiety. In the search for knowledge of the outcome of a particular case of sickness a royal patient might send abroad to the temple of a foreign god, though perhaps not until the resources of some local Yahweh shrine had been exhausted. Among a people to whom such maladies as came upon them and their friends were evidence of divine displeasure, there was little to do save to attempt to remove that displeasure. Yet they were not utterly without nurses to care for the sick, but these, as the terms used suggest, were usually employed in the care of mothers at childbirth and of the children in the home. The well nigh omnipresent female slave was usually available and must not infrequently have been possessed of considerable skill in caring for the sick. Ignorance of dietary rules is shown by the kind of food sometimes administered to the patient. We wonder whether the sick and famished man of whom we read survived the two raisin cakes and the piece of fig cake which

were fed him.[1]   Where the sickness was severe and
death seemed inevitable, no attempt was made to
prolong life unnecessarily ; a man's right to die was
recognised.

The neglect of the patient, so common in those
times, and so distressing to us as we contemplate it,
should not be considered as evidencing a want of
affection ; though the conviction that Yahweh had
afflicted or sickened the patient because of some offence committed by him, would in many instances
leave friends in a doubtful state of mind.   On the
other hand, the violent way in which the intelligence
of death or calamity was received should not lead us
to suppose that these people were extraordinarily
fond of each other and endowed in an unusual degree
with deep feeling.   The custom of tearing the outer
garment as a sign of grief was undoubtedly of great
antiquity and was not without its significance and
appropriateness, shocking as it may seem to us with
our less demonstrative sensibilities and our ideas of
decency and self-restraint.   And such expressions of
grief were not, we have to notice, isolated.   If the
head of a family tore his outer robe, the other members, male and female, did likewise ; if the King thus
gave expression to his suddenly aroused feeling, all
members of the Court must follow his sad example.
Sometimes, indeed, a whole city would thus give vent
to their sorrow caused by some public calamity, as
when the King's household was afflicted.   A coarse
cloth known as *saq* (שׂק), whence perhaps through the

---

[1] As the Septuagint omits the raisin cakes, we may surmise they
were not originally mentioned in the Hebrew text.

Greek our own term sack, would be donned as a symbol of grief, while dust or ashes would be liberally
sprinkled upon the head. So easily and so frequently
were people thrown into these violent exhibitions of
grief that it seems to us as though the noise of rip-
ping garments must ever have been heard. It is possible that some seam was left in a ripable state; if
not, seams must have multiplied upon the garments
of most men with alarming rapidity. One of the
verbs used of mourning very commonly (אבל) conveys
the thought of drooping or fading, but the more common (ספד) means to beat or to smite, and suggests to
us what was true of the people, that they often severely afflicted themselves when in mourning.

Yet, violent as the exhibitions of grief were on the
part of friends, the afflicted did not do all their wailing. Hired mourners, of whom we read in Jesus'
day, were apparently employed then. That grief
over the loss of some dear one seemed to the afflicted friend well nigh unbearable, we need not wonder
if we stop to reflect that the place of their departed
in their thought was Sheol, the cheerless underworld.
No least expression of a hope of a better environment beyond for their departed have we in the literature of this period. Even in the beautiful dirge
which David is said to have composed, a lament
over Saul and Jonathan, there is not only no expression of a larger hope, but there is also wanting
the marks of a religious character. No religious
note is there; even Yahweh himself is not mentioned. Still, though they thus regarded the transition known as death, the departed were kept in re-

membrance. By the Hebrews, bodies of valorous men of war sometimes, if not usually, were, as among the Greeks, burnt upon a funeral pyre;[1] and the bones sacredly collected and stones piled high upon them.[2] Thus were such men long kept in remembrance. Costly tombs were often constructed, and limestone caves in some parts of the land were appropriately used. Some in their life-time reared monuments to perpetuate their memory. Such was Absalom's monument erected by him a considerable time before his death in the King's dale near Jerusalem.

[1] 1 Sam. xxxi. 12; cf. Smith, *Samuel, I. C.*, p. 253.
[2] 2 Sam. xviii. 17.

CHAPTER XII

THE PURIFICATION OF YAHWISM

WORTHY of serious thought is the epigram of one who up to the time of his death was a pronounced and prominent opponent of Christianity, blasphemous as at first it seemed to us : " An honest god is the noblest work of man." One is reminded of this as he traces the development of Yahwism among the Hebrews. The Eternal God with whom we all have to do is never to be confounded with any nation's conception of Him.[1] Though He may seek in many ways to reveal himself to a people, their god as he is proclaimed by them, and especially as he is set forth in their early literature, is their thought of what God is, which is never to be confounded with the Absolute Being. This is eminently true of the Yahweh of the Hebrews. As we patiently study their literature and seek to know them, we find certain conceptions of God as they apprehended Him. It is for us to account for these imperfect conceptions and to trace the effects of these upon their social life. We have not to do with the idea of " the Divine Being accommodating Himself " to a people on their way up out of a low stage of culture; we have to do

[1] Budde, *Rel. of Is. to the Ex.*, p. 1, note; (Wellhausen) *Encyc. Brit.*, vol. xiii., p. 399.

with Yahwism. The low moral standards, the passion, and the hard, cruel, and unreasonable arbitrariness belong to Yahwism; and the leaving of these imperfections behind and the emergence of a lofty ethical standard and of an inspiring universalism such as we find in Amos, Hosea, Isaiah, and Micah, can be accounted for if we note the ethical development of the best type of life among the Hebrews. Yahwism never far surpassed this. Often, as in the earlier time, it seems to have fallen behind it, and it is to be feared that at its best in the eighth century it did not have a very salutary influence upon the social life of the people as a whole, for the Yahwism as the mass of the people understood it was quite different from Yahwism as their great prophets understood it.

In the time of David and long after, as in the earlier time, Yahweh was conceived as a war-god. He glories in carnage and leads his people against neighbouring nations with no manifestation of interest in or of pity for them. In time of battle he gives his voice, *i.e.*, he thunders,[1] and thus encourages his people and discomfits the enemy. If on occasion his people are vanquished, if they flee before their enemies and are slaughtered it is because he in his fickleness or his jealousy has felt slighted. There may, indeed, have been committed some offence, not of an immoral character as we understand it, but something rather in the way of failure to perform an ancient ritualistic practice. The fat of a victim

[1] 1 Sam. vii. 10; 2 Sam. xxii. 14; Is. xxix. 6; cf. 1 Sam. ii. 10; Psalm xviii. 13; xxix. 3.

slaughtered at a high place has not been burnt for him, or the blood has not been poured out, or a priest at a local sanctuary has overridden time-honoured customs and has so discouraged the people that the worship of that particular sanctuary has well nigh ceased, or, it may be, the keeper of a shrine has sent them against the enemy when the omens were unfavourable.   Such acts as these rather than oppression of the poor and murder of the innocent were in that earlier time, in their thought, the causes which stirred up Yahweh to wrath and provoked him to bring confusion upon them.

Sickness and pestilence and calamities of other kinds were, as we have seen, attributed to Yahweh. They were of his sending and were often traced, as was failure in a campaign against an enemy, to some offence committed by them that Yahweh could not condone.   The supposed offence may seem innocent enough to us where it was nothing more than the enrolment of the fighting men; but when it was the violation of a covenant with a neighbouring people there was reason, as we can see, for thinking Yahweh, in whose name covenants were made and who watched over these sacred compacts, to be aggrieved whenever they failed to live up to their covenant obligations.   That he should have been conceived of as requiring the blood of members of a family the head of which had in his treatment of a people broken a covenant made with them, we can understand, but we can also easily see how such a king as David might plead the necessity of avenging, in Yahweh's name, the violation of an old covenant as excuse for destroying the male members of a rival house. We have no sadder example of the cruel side of the Yahwism of those times than is presented in the slaughterings of Jehu, who in his zeal for Yahweh which was stimulated by Elisha, involved, according to the chronicler, North Israel in a carnival of blood, in which the innocent apparently went down with the guilty. That Jehu was utterly wanting in the common principles of humanity and that his conduct was wholly selfish and vengeful seems indisputable. Elisha mistook his man. He chose in Jehu one utterly unfit to right abuses and unfit to reign after having tried to right them; yet he seems not to have discovered anything offensive to Yahwism in the high-handed and bloody way in which Jehu conducted himself.[1] Yahwism as he understood it was easily reconcilable with such conduct. Perhaps it was this side of the prophet and his proverbial disposition to consider Yahweh as vengeful, that explains the she-bear story, with which his name is unpleasantly associated. Such misconceptions of God's character as thus appear in the Yahwism of those times necessarily wrought disastrously. They made themselves unhappily felt upon the social life of the people. A strong, pure society was impossible so long as such thoughts of the Divine Being inspired or controlled the conduct of men. At times, we must believe, a man's sense of right triumphed, his humane sentiments got the better of him, and he did what he felt to be right regardless of consequences. Usually, however, it was otherwise; and much of the moral

[1] Budde, *Rel. of Is. to the Ex.*, p. 124 ff.

obliquity which we discover among the Hebrews of the monarchy must be charged to Yahwism, though for the character of Yahwism they were themselves at least partially responsible. It was of their own making, and though superior in many respects to the religion of other peoples of antiquity, it had its great limitations and imperfections that made themselves powerfully felt upon the social life of the people.

The limitations in the Hebrew conception of Yahweh as God appear in the anthropomorphisms of those times. Here, probably, we are not as in the later time to think of mere figures of speech as when we are told that Yahweh amused himself at the expense of the Egyptians, or that he sitteth in the heavens and laughs at the confusion of the heathen. The J narrative of creation speaks of Yahweh as forming man and the beasts out of the dust of the ground, etc., because the writers of it could not think of him as making man in any other way. The cosmogony of J belongs to the thought of the time. In few respects does it rise superior to it.

But if the basal conceptions of Yahwism were at fault and were unfortunate in their influence upon the people, quite as surely were the ways in which Yahweh was gratified or appeased, or the ways in which his will or wish was ascertained socially demoralising. Wine and blood were poured out to him and fat was burnt for his gratification as in the earlier time. Such offerings were conceived of as peculiarly pleasing to him. The old sanctuaries continued in favour and were certainly used until Josiah's day; they probably were much later. High places increased as the population increased and spread over the land. Altars and shrines were under many a great oak and terebinth. At the prominent sanctuaries the one great annual feast was still observed; at these and at the high places, social gatherings of a minor character were often held, when the people feasted with their god and made merry, pouring out the blood and burning the fat to Yahweh as his portion. Wine was thus offered, and under certain circumstances water might be poured out. If a prince gave a feast to his companions he took them to some sacrificial stone or holy place. Absalom went with his friends to Hebron and worshipped there the Yahweh of Hebron. Adonijah took the King's sons to the stone of Zoheleth. Sometimes, it is true, when there seemed to be special reason for it, cattle were slaughtered where they chanced to be, the wood of the yoke and of the threshing-sledge or wagon being used for the sacrificial fire.

Human sacrifices, of which there are abundant traces up to the time of the Exile, were common in this as in the earlier period. In accordance with the custom of the people of their time, or in obedience to some vow, captives taken in war, personal enemies and even members of one's own family, were offered by pious Hebrews. It was only in the late literature of the prophets that the practice was denounced. The story of Abraham's unfulfilled sacrifice of Isaac belongs to the time of the monarchy. In the early literature there was no thought of suggesting a substitute, unless it be that the law in Exodus xiii. 13 ff.

and xxxiv. 20 ff. is early, which seems improbable,[1] and that the victim substituted for Jonathan when he by touching and eating food upon which a taboo had been placed became himself taboo, was an animal instead of a human being. Jephthah's daughter was sacrificed ; so also were the seventy sons of Jerubbaal. The frequent mention of human sacrifices during this period, which has an astonishingly large number of references to them, should not be contrasted with the less frequent mention of them in the earlier literature, for the probability is that the earlier period witnessed such sacrifices with even greater frequency. The devotion of a family or of a community to Yahweh and their consequent destruction is to be included under this head as in the nature of human sacrifices. Thus at the time of the settlement a few, at least, of the weaker cities inhabited by the Canaanites may have been, as they fell into the hands of the Hebrews, so devoted as appears to have been the case later. Nothing in the character of the Yahwism of the time now under consideration is more revolting to us than the thought that the Hebrews could unblushingly conceive of Yahweh as wishing to drink the blood of such victims. Yet this is something that may not be overlooked if we wish to determine the influence of Yahwism upon their social life.

---

[1] That this law was a part of J and that in its origin it may be considerably older than the ninth century may be readily admitted so far as it had to do with the first-born of man. That it did not forbid human sacrifices under certain circumstances should, however, be recognised.

The medium by which the will of Yahweh was determined until the prophets came to the front was the sacred lot which was employed in the earlier time. Necessarily its decisions were of an arbitrary and erratic character. Just what the lot was and just how it was taken we cannot say, though we may surmise with some degree of probability. There is frequent mention in the earlier literature of ephod-idols which are now thought to have been images of Yahweh, while in the later time the ephod appears to have been made of linen and to have been worn. That the ephod of the time of Saul and David was what it was earlier is disguised by our translators, who speak of it as being worn when the Hebrew text and the Septuagint both use the verb " to bear," which cannot reasonably be interpreted to refer to the wearing of anything.[1] In the earlier time Gideon made for himself an ephod-idol. Micah also had one. Upon two occasions David during his wandering life is known to have called for the ephod-idol. These images were carried at a later day in time of battle, probably in the Ark. If they were not identified with Yahweh and worshipped, they were certainly held in peculiar esteem. The sacred lot appears to have been cast before them. This was the purpose for which David desired the ephod on the occasions just mentioned. In the first instance he wished to know if Saul would come down and if the men of Keilah could be trusted.[2] The sacred lot decided the first

---

[1] It is probable that in the later literature the verb was more loosely used.

[2] Samuel xxiii. 2.

question affirmatively, the second negatively. In the second instance David desired to know whether if he pursued the Amalekites he should overtake them and secure the booty which they had gotten. Here again the lot was affirmative. Similarly, the five Danites of a much earlier time inquired through a Levite when on a prospecting tour to ascertain whether their journey would be propitious.[1] An affirmative answer, corroborated by the sequel, so prejudiced the Danites in favour of this man and the sanctuary of Micah which he served as minister, that they later, when migrating northward, seized and took with them the ephod and other images together with the attendant, leaving Micah, in so doing, in tears. Just how the lot, which was by Urim and Thummim before the ephod-idol, was taken, we cannot say positively. Apparently, as Dr. Smith suggests, the Urim and Thummim were pebbles,[2] one of which may have been white, the other coloured, so that one gave the affirmative and the other the negative. The sacred lot was long and largely used among the Hebrews of all classes, both in ordinary and in extraordinary affairs, and seems to have been received with well nigh universal favour despite the fact that mere chance played so large a place in its decisions. We must not allow ourselves to be misled by such phrases as "inquired of Yahweh," or "asked Yahweh," into supposing that the request was made in the form of audible or inaudible prayer. It was the sacred lot which was used. Prayer as we understand it was not made during the

---

[1] Judges xviii. 5.
[2] H. P. Smith, *Samuel*, *I. C.*, p. 122.

earlier centuries under consideration. Something in
the nature of an invocation there might be when a
man put his hand to some task of great magnitude,
as: "May Yahweh be gracious," or "May Yahweh
give success;" while at sanctuaries a vow might serve
as a prayer, as when Hannah is said to have prayed.
A new day dawned upon Israel when men of God of
irreproachable character came to the front and offered
themselves as interpreters of the will of Yahweh.
Such men might make mistakes occasionally; but
there could never be about their decisions the irre-
sponsible character that there was about the sacred
lot. Here, too, it must be admitted, was an opportunity for selfish, characterless men to exploit both
king and people; such men did actually appear.
They wrought great injury as false prophets. But
the high-souled man as an interpreter of the will of
Yahweh had, as we have intimated, an important
and beneficent mission that was most happy in its
effects upon society. Such men belonged to the
purified Yahwism of the eighth century, which appears to have been the possession of a few favoured
ones.

Aside from the stories of the worship of Baal and
Astarte in the north when Jezebel, the Tyrian prin-
cess,[1] came forward as their patron, the actual records of these centuries give us little concerning these
foreign cults, for we must reject the pragmatism of
the Deuteronomist in the Books of the Kings. This
is surprising, for we cannot believe that Baal and
Astarte so soon ceased to dispute with Yahweh the

[1] Budde, *Rel. of Is. to the Ex.*, p. 116 ff.

possession of the land and the service of the people. It is singular that the Books of the Chronicles furnish us a key to the situation. Certain names which appear in Chronicles, as Ishbaal, the name of a son of Saul, Meribaal, the name of a son of Jonathan, Baaliada, a son of David, etc., reveal that Baal was long held in honour among the Hebrews. The fact that these names appear in 2 Samuel as Ishbosheth, Mephibosheth, Eliada, etc.—impossible names in the first two instances at least for fathers to give their sons—raises on our part the query whether the Books of Samuel did not have erased from them well nigh all traces of the worship of Baal and Astarte. The wretched condition of the texts of these books as they now stand may be considered an argument in favour of this. Surely a hand that could thus change the names of prominent individuals could also work over or delete passages. That Yahweh, as the Hebrews increased in numbers and importance and absorbed the old Canaanites, came to be regarded as the God of the land is evident, though there are reasons for believing that at most of the high places and sanctuaries Baal and Astarte were worshipped more or less until the Exile.

As we come down into the days of the earlier prophets, who have left us in writing some fragments of their work, we marvel not more over the exalted conception of Yahweh which they present us than we do over their insistence upon an ethical code that must have been much in advance of their day.[1] That

[1] Budde, *Rel. of Is. to the Ex.*, p. 127 ff.

it was far from being practised among their people
we know. Their warnings and denunciations make
this evident enough. We have, however, to recognise
the fact that the J and E narratives which appear to
have come from men of the prophetic type of mind
who antedated Amos and Hosea a half century or
more, give us, with all their anthropomorphisms
and inadequate moral conceptions of Yahweh, a loftier range of thought than we find in 2 Samuel and
1 Kings.

According to Amos, Yahweh is still the thunderer;
he is also the one who smites with blasting and mildew garden and orchard and vineyard; who sends the
palmer-worm and the locust, and who causes the pastures of the shepherds to mourn and the top of Carmel
to wither. He is more: as creator he formed light
and created darkness, he shaped the mountains and
brought forth the winds. As controller among the
nations he guided the migrations of the olden time
and watched over the destinies of Israel. Nor is this
the whole story, for Yahweh is he from whom nothing
has been hidden, and who has seen and punished
iniquity, sending his afflictive judgments, locust and
palmer-worm and pestilence and other calamity; but
who has also raised up Nazarite and prophet, revealing to the latter his secret councils in his endeavour
to succour and save his people. As one who loves the
right and hates the evil, he cannot overlook injustice
nor let inhumanity go unpunished. He is not to be
propitiated by sacrifices; they are an offence to him.
The worship of the sanctuaries, with their vain din,
their lewdness and drunkenness and extortion, he

utterly abhors.   The taking of bribes, the oppression
of the poor and the denial of justice to the needy, the
selling of the righteous into slavery and the inhumanity of the rich, he must punish.   Luxurious idleness
he loathes ; even, such is his love of simplicity,
houses of hewn stone and ivory palaces please him
not.   Inhumanity both within and without Israel
Yahweh will punish, bringing upon great and conspicuous offenders an awful doom.   Other outrageous
sinners are to be brought to confusion—into captivity
they must go.   Yet Yahweh is gracious ; and a remnant of Joseph will upon reformation be spared.

To Hosea, Yahweh's interests were local.   As the
God of Israel he devotes himself to Israel.   His lov-
ing care has been with them from of old, when he
made choice of them and brought them forth.   He
has shown himself tenderly and lovingly pitiful as he
has borne with the infidelity of his people in his
hope that he might bring them back to their old allegiance.   In his endeavour to save his people he has
sought to hedge up their way and to restrain them
rather than to afflict.   If he has torn, it has been
that he might heal.   That his people might return to
him and do righteously ; that they might show mercy
in the common relations of life rather than multiply
sacrifices at their sanctuaries and high places, he has
affectionately dealt with them.   Such dealing on his
part has found no reciprocation on their part.   From
bad to worse they have gone, until even priest and
prophet are involved in the common ruin.   The
wealth of Ephraim is not to save him ; political en-
tanglements will but render more inevitable the evil

day. Among them there is no truth, nor is there mercy, knowledge of God is wanting; false swearing, the breaking of covenant obligations, theft, adultery, and murder abound; divination, drunkenness, and lewdness at high places and under sacred trees are also to be charged to them. All this, in view of the past pitifulness of Yahweh, necessitates on his part severe discipline. Destruction must come upon them. Vain, proud Ephraim must come to naught; as the morning cloud, as the smoke of a chimney, he must pass away; even the land must mourn; all nature must languish. Yet even here there is, as the prophet pleads with an incorrigible people, hope of a brighter day if they but repentantly return.

The prophecies of Micah should be considered in connection with the work of Hosea. He closely followed him; his discourses abound in references to the people of the north, especially Samaria, the doom of which seemed to be impending; he also, like his predecessor, was keenly sensitive to social wrongs. Yahweh to him was an exalted being before whom mountains melt and valleys are cleft; but it was not so much these aspects of Yahweh that appealed to him as it was his determination to purify society and obliterate old lines of cleavage. Sacrifices he desires not; they are a weariness to him. In order to please him men must do justly, love mercy, and walk humbly. This the men of his day were not doing. The rich were full of violence; and deceit was in the mouth of all. Those in authority abhorred judgment and prevented equity; while all were haters of good and lovers of evil. By night upon their beds men devised the evil they were to practise during the day. Fields they coveted and seized. The most helpless, the women and the children, were cast out; and inhuman deeds were practised on all sides, though nowhere more openly and impiously than in Samaria. In Micah's thought a day of reckoning could not be avoided. It would come, bringing destruction to graven images and their worshippers; to "devoted women" and to sanctuaries. Not only would they sow and fail to reap, tread olives and fail to anoint themselves, tread grapes and fail to drink of the wine; but the people would also suffer from the hand of the devastator. But this same prophet has a bright picture of the good time coming when in the latter day Yahweh's house was to be established in his hill, and as the nations were brought under his hand universal righteousness and peace were to prevail. Under him a new prince was to arise who was to shepherd his people gently and lovingly.

With greater fulness and with richer imagery does Isaiah appear before us manifesting the same interest in social well-being and revealing the same lofty type of Yahwism. To him, Yahweh is one who is to arise to strike terror in the earth; one from whose splendour and majesty a disobedient people should hide themselves. In his own experience he had seen him seated upon a throne, high and lifted up, before whom cherubim stood. In sight of such a one incorrigible sinners cannot indefinitely disport themselves. By his fury he will burn up their land. Against them he has stirred up foreign foes. Yet Yahweh is one who has planted a vineyard, and has lavished upon it affectionately his care, though to no purpose, for it has brought forth naught but wild grapes. Such was the condition of things socially from 740 B.C. onward for nearly forty years, the period covered by this prophet, that he saw no hope of salvation save in a righteous remnant. The rottenness of the mass did not escape the observation of a man who lived in the midst of it, and had daily to do with it. Idolatry, drunkenness, and lewdness were still rife at the high places and sanctuaries. Diviners from the East and soothsayers from the Philistines made spoil of the people. Those who were but youths served as princes and insulting boys lorded it over them. And these ground the face of the poor, crushed the needy, and spoiled those possessed of means. The wealthy women of Jerusalem were vain, dressy, gay, artful, and characterless. Yet was the land, at least in the earlier days of this prophet, rich in silver and in gold, in horses and in chariots. This, however, led not to contentment, for even the rich sought to add field to field, and house to house. It may be that we have here in Isaiah of the capital as we have in Amos of the meagre region to the southeast of Jerusalem an ascetic note that is not altogether healthful; but that the society of his day was wretchedly bad we must believe. Worst of all was the fact that moral distinctions were obscured so that men called, perhaps unwittingly, evil good, and darkness light. The value of these prophets to their people was not so much in the actual reforms which they inaugurated, for they appear to have had comparatively little influence upon their own time, as in that they clarified

the minds of the few and by their clear distinctions
and high ideals prepared the way for the new day
which they all believed would follow upon the sifting
which the people would get through Yahweh's disciplinary afflictions.

We may think of these prophets as having their
forerunners in the "men of Yahweh," or "men of
Elohim," who appear before us in the earlier period
but dimly.   Or we may think of the wild enthusiasts
of Saul's time as in some sense their forerunners.
This is even more doubtful as a supposition.   It
seems more reasonable to think of such men as
Elijah and Elisha and Micaiah ben Imlah by whom
Yahweh spake in the days of Ahab of North Israel,
and Jonah ben Amittai by whom Yahweh addressed
Jeroboam II., as the real predecessors of the prophets whose discourses we have.   And these earlier
prophets named above must have been closely in
touch with the schools known to us as J and E.
Some of them were very likely members of it.

Nowhere in the literature of this period do we find
trace of the doctrine of evil spirits that appeared in
Jewish literature after Persian influence made itself
felt.   Good spirits are mentioned as associated with
Yahweh.   Through these he frequently accomplishes
his purposes, putting at times words of deceit upon
their tongues that he may misguide men.   It is probable that the thought of evil spirits, and more particularly of Satan, came to the Jewish mind as furnishing some sort of relief, dissatisfied as it was
then getting over its conception of Yahweh.   In the
purified Yahwism of the prophets there was no need

of it. Had the thought of Amos, Hosea, Isaiah, and Micah been heartily espoused, foreign influence would have found small place in later Jewish thought. But the hearty espousal of their thought would have affected even more beneficently the social life of their own and of later generations.

CHAPTER XIII

THE CONCLUSION

THE writer of this volume, after seeing the Tissot pictures or illustrations of the life of Jesus in New York, compared experiences with an estimable Christian woman who has travelled in the Holy Land. During the course of the conversation he put to her the question he had wished someone to answer: "What about the rich, even high, Venetian colouring of the pictures; can it be that they are true to life, to local colour? Palestine surely can never have had so much colour?" "Yes," was the reply, "Tissot is true to life here. Most Eastern buildings are a dingy white, but such is the witchery of light in that practically cloudless land that the charm of colour is thrown over everything, beautifying and glorifying all."[1]

The reader of this book, if he has had the patience to push through its pages, has followed an honest and painstaking attempt to depict the social life of the Hebrews; but he has looked at dim, colourless pencil sketches, not a series of richly or brilliantly

[1] The answer given to this question as to colour has not been verified. It is singular to what extent travellers in Palestine have allowed the archæological sense to determine the character of their work. Artists with an eye for local colour may after all in some particulars be our best interpreters of Eastern life.

coloured prints. Hints here and there he has found
that have enabled him, if possessed of considerable
imagination, to discover a little local colour and so to
gain a glimpse of the real life of the people. The first
period is one that marked a readjustment of the Hebrew clans, a settlement in the midst of a new ethnographical and geographical environment, into which,
unbidden and unwelcomed, they had made their way
and for which they were willing to fight. In some way
they had been weaned from and outgrown the desert
and nomadic life and made willing, even though
to them their Yahweh was the God of the sublime
southern mountains and its desert solitudes, to ad-
venture, prepared for enterprise. Perhaps already
their moral and intellectual values had increased beyond the nomadic stage.[1] So it seems to us, but
however this may have been, we know that they cannot have possessed a strong consciousness of the
land into which they went as peculiarly theirs. It
may even be questioned whether they had any traditions of ancient progenitors who had wandered
therein. Even if they had such traditions they
could hardly have thought of them as a warrant for
claiming the soil of Canaan, for the conception of
property in land then prevalent would hardly have
allowed this. Right to land was largely summed up
in the question of possession ; and the Canaanites
held Canaan ; their local Baalim were the proprietors of the soil. But having gone in and having
made themselves fairly at home therein, the Hebrews soon secured a competence and made them-

[1] Hastings' *Dictionary*, vol. ii., p. 820.

selves comfortable as they also in time made themselves feared if not respected. And they were not long in developing a love for the land which was really vastly superior to that which they had left behind. They came to glory in its hills and vales, its lakes and water-courses, its distant mountains and its more distant sea.

The period which we have studied in our second part has proved much richer, not merely because of the more abundant literature which it has passed on to us, but also because it presents to us a higher and more complex type of civilisation. What appears in the germ in the earlier period appears in this, in its fruitage; and though in its perfected form it may disappoint us, it surely has more interest for us than can be found in its less developed forms. Life as lived in this later stage was lived under monarchies. These though small, and it may be just because they were small and so within the sphere of vision of most of the people, gave life most of its colour. The people could not forget that they lived under such rulers. In little ways they were being continually reminded of this overlordship, sometimes unpleasantly, at other times most pleasantly. Life had meanwhile for many lost its meagre and strenuous character. There were greater opportunities for leisure and more to interest men when unoccupied with the sterner things of life. There was on the whole, moreover, less insecurity. The Canaanites were becoming a part of them; they were no longer to be feared. The Hebrews could think of themselves as destined to become, if not already, the real possessors of the land.

With this growing consciousness there came inevitably a conviction that their Yahweh was, after all, a superior God. This prepared them for the assertions of the universality of Yahweh, a doctrine that was to survive the purifying fires of the Captivity before it could reach its best fruitage.

But what of the actual life lived therein; was it to them interesting and joyous? Preëminently so. Life was not colourless, it rather was full of colour, though not without its arduous toil, its struggles and its sacrifices. Somehow these people found even in heroic effort and in conflict a peculiar satisfaction. Children of the East, they yet were not effeminate. Even to this day the Jewish stock is full of vigour, not so much because there has been incorporation from without, though it is undoubtedly true that no Jewish blood is pure, as because the original vitality has not spent itself.

A study of the social life of the Hebrews of these periods reminds one of the early Greek life, described so vividly and fascinatingly by the Homeridæ, a life practically contemporaneous with this. Into the plains one must go to find the more important paraphernalia of war as the iron-bound chariot with its driver, its shield-bearer, and its warrior, drawn by prancing steeds which smelt the battle from afar and joyed therein; yet among the hills one finds spearmen as well as bowmen, dwelling for the most part in walled cities and possessed of most of the utilities of their time. Life was as strenuous as among the Greeks and certainly as joyous and undoubtedly even more hopeful, for re-

ligion meant more to the Hebrews than it did to
the Greeks.

It is matter for keen regret that most of the early
Hebrew poetry was lost. While rejoicing in the folk-
tales and the chronicles without which we could not
reproduce that old life, we still feel the loss of the
greater part of the early poetry. So richly suggestive are the Song of Deborah, the Dirge of David
over Saul and Jonathan, and the later Blessing of
Jacob and that of Moses, and a few other poems that
might be named, that we cannot avoid remarking that
had the Hebrews preserved all that they produced in
the way of poetry, the task of reproducing their past
would be immeasurably easier than it is. The few
fragments which we have reveal much. The war-
ode of Deborah, than which there is probably none
in any literature superior, is itself a storehouse of
invaluable data. With a few score of such poems,
which the Hebrews once possessed in oral if not in
written form, we should find it as easy to reconstruct
the actual life of this people as we do in the case
of the early Greeks. But this was not to be. With
such materials as we have we must reconstruct, getting hints from now a word, now an allusion, now
an ancient custom which is incidentally mentioned;
until we come to the chronicles, which, rich as they
are in the material they give, can never make good
to us the loss of the old poetry which sprang out of
the very life of the people, and must, if we may
judge from the few fragments of it which remain,
have been warm with the blood of their throbbing
hearts. If in this labour of reconstructing the social

life of the Hebrews of those times, this volume shall prove to have helped, a labour which has been increasingly a delight as the months have passed, will be a joy even in retrospect despite the certainty of almost daily discovery of the need of correction or of revision at some point.

APPENDIX

I

HARMONY OF PASSAGES RELATING TO THE SETTLEMENT

THE FIRST MIGRATION

The Settlement of the Southern Highlands and the Negeb

JUDGES i. 1–7

(And it came to pass after the death of Joshua)[1] that the children of Israel inquired of Yahweh, saying : Who shall go up first against the Canaanites, to fight against them? And Yahweh answered : Judah shall go up ; behold, I will give the land into his hand. And Judah said unto Simeon his brother : Go up with me into my lot, that we may make war against the Canaanites ; and then I will go with you into your lot. So Simeon went with him. And Judah went up ; and

Compare with this the wonderful story as told in Joshua x. 1–14, which belongs to P, and has, therefore, as a late narrative, little, if any, foundation in fact.

[1] The parts enclosed belong to late editors. See Moore, *Judges, Polychrome.*

Yahweh delivered the Ca-
naanites (and the Perizzites
into their hand : and they
smote of them in Bezek ten
thousand men).   And they
found Adoni-bezek in Bezek:
and they fought against
him, and they smote the
Canaanites (and the Perizzites).   And   Adoni-bezek
fled ; and they pursued after
him, and caught him, and
cut off his thumbs and his
great toes.   And Adoni-bezek said: Seventy kings,
having their thumbs and
their great toes cut off,
gathered their meat under
my table : as I have done,
so God hath requited me.
And they brought him to
Jerusalem, and he   died
there.

JUDGES i. 8

(And the children of Ju-
dah fought against Jerusalem, and took it, and smote
it with the edge of the
sword, and destroyed the
city with fire.)

JOSHUA xv. 63

And as for the Jebusites,
the inhabitants of Jerusalem, the children of Judah
could not drive them out :
but the Jebusites dwelt with
the children of Judah at
Jerusalem, unto this day.

JUDGES i. 21

And the children of Benjamin did not drive out the
Jebusites that inhabited Jerusalem ; but the Jebusites
dwelt with the children of Benjamin, in Jerusalem, unto
this day.

JUDGES i. 9

And afterward the children of Judah went down to fight against the Canaanites that dwelt in the highlands, and in the South (and in the Shephelah).

JUDGES i. 17–19

And Judah went with Simeon his brother, and they smote the Canaanites that inhabited Zephath, and utterly destroyed it. And the name of the city was called Hormah. (Also Judah took Gaza with the border thereof, and Askelon, with the border thereof, and Ekron with the border thereof.)

And Yahweh was with Judah; and he drove out the inhabitants of the highlands; for he could not drive out the inhabitants of the plain, because they had iron chariots.

JUDGES i. 10, 20, 11–15	JOSHUA xv. 14–19
(And Judah went against the Canaanites that dwelt in Hebron: now the name of Hebron beforetime was Kiriath-arba:) and they smote Hebron and gave it unto Caleb, as Moses had spoken: and he drove out thence the three sons of Anak, Sheshai, and Ahiman, and Talmai. And from thence he went up against the inhabitants of Debir. Now the name of Debir beforetime was Kiriath-sepher. And Caleb said: He that smiteth Kiriath-sepher, and taketh it, to him will I give Achsah my daughter to	And Caleb drove out thence the three sons of Anak, Sheshai, and Ahiman, and Talmai, the sons of Anak. And he went up thence against the inhabitants of Debir: now the name of Debir beforetime was Kiriath-sepher. And Caleb said: He that smiteth Kiriath-sepher, and taketh it, to him will I give Achsah my daughter to wife. And Othniel the son of Kenaz, the brother of Caleb, took it: and he gave him Achsah his daughter to wife. And it came to pass, when she came unto him, that he

wife. And Othniel the son of Kenaz, Caleb's younger brother, took it : and he gave him Achsah his daughter to wife. And it came to pass, when she came unto him, that he moved her to ask of her father a field : and she lighted from off her ass ; and Caleb said unto her : What wouldst thou ? And she said unto him : Give me a present ; for thou hast set me in the land of the South, give me also springs of water. And Caleb gave her the upper springs and the nether springs.

moved her to ask of her father a field : and she lighted down from off her ass ; and Caleb said unto her : What wouldst thou ? And she said : give me a present ; for that thou hast set me in the land of the South, give me also springs of water. And he gave her the upper springs and the nether springs.

JUDGES i. 16

And Hobab the Kenite, Moses' brother-in-law, went up out of the city of palm-trees with the children of Judah into the wilderness of Judah, which is in the south of Arad ; and he went and dwelt with Amalek. And the border of the Edomites [1] was from the ascent of Akrabbim, from the rock and upward.

THE SECOND MIGRATION

The Settlement of the Central Highlands

JUDGES i. 22-26

And the house of Joseph, they also went up against Bethel : and Yahweh was

(Compare with this simple story the more fanciful one found in Joshua viii. 1-29.

[1] This emendation of the text suggested by Dr. Moore is undoubtedly correct.

with them. And the house
of Joseph sent to spy out
Bethel. (Now the name of
the city was beforetime Luz.)
And the watches saw a man
come forth out of the city,
and they said unto him :
Show us, we pray thee, the
entrance into the city, and we
will deal kindly with thee.
And he shewed them the
entrance into the city, and
they smote the city with the
edge of the sword ; but they
sent away the man and all
of his family. And the man
went into the land of the
Hittites, and built a city,
and called the name thereof
Luz ; which is the name
thereof unto this day.

Notice also as a supplement
of the Judges story Joshua
xvii. 14–18.)

JUDGES i. 27, 28

And Manasseh did not
drive out the inhabitants of
Beth-shean and her depen-
dencies, nor the inhabitants
of Taanach and her depen-
dencies, nor the inhabitants
of Dor and her dependen-
cies, nor the inhabitants of
Ibleam and her dependen-
cies, nor the inhabitants
of Megiddo and her depen-
dencies : but the Canaan-
ites stubbornly dwelt in
that country. And it came

JOSHUA xvii. 11–13

And Manasseh had in Is-
sachar and in Asher Beth-
shean and her dependencies,
and Ibleam and her depen-
dencies, and the inhabitants
of Dor and her dependencies,
and the inhabitants of Endor and her dependencies,
and the inhabitants of Taanach and her dependencies,
and the inhabitants of Megiddo and her dependencies,
even the three heights. Yet
the children of Manasseh

to pass, when Israel was waxen strong, that they put the Canaanites to task-work, and did not utterly drive them out.

could not drive out the inhabitants of those cities; but the Canaanites stubbornly dwelt in the land. And it came to pass when the children of Israel were waxen strong, that they put the Canaanites to task-work, and did not utterly drive them out.

JUDGES i. 29

And Ephraim drove not out the Canaanites that dwelt in Gezer; but the Canaanites dwelt in Gezer among them.

JOSHUA xvi. 10

And they (*i.e.*, Ephraim) drove not out the Canaanites that dwelt in Gezer: but the Canaanites dwelt in the midst of Ephraim unto this day.

The Migrations and Settlement of Dan

JUDGES i. 34, 35

And the Amorites forced the children of Dan into the highlands: for they would not suffer them to come down into the plain: but the Amorites stubbornly dwelt in Mount Heres, in Aijalon, and in Shaalbim: yet the hand of the house of Joseph prevailed, so that they became tributary.

(Joshua xix. 47 has a brief account of the settlement of Dan in the North at Leshem, *i.e.*, Laish. Compare this with Judges xviii.)

THE THIRD MIGRATION

The Settlement of the North

JUDGES i. 30–33

Zebulun drove not out the inhabitants of Kitron, nor the inhabitants of Nahalol ; but the Canaanites dwelt among them, and became tributary.

Asher drove not out the inhabitants of Acco, nor the inhabitants of Zidon, nor of Ahlab, nor of Achzib, nor of Helbah, nor of Aphik, nor of Rehob : but the Asherites dwelt among the Canaanites, the inhabitants of the land : for they did not drive them out.

Naphtali drove not out the inhabitants of Beth-shemesh, nor the inhabitants of Beth-anath ; but dwelt among the Canaanites, the inhabitants of the land ; nevertheless the inhabitants of Beth-shemesh and of Beth-anath became tributary unto them.

The Canaanites Unexterminated

JUDGES ii. 23

So Yahweh left these peoples, not dispossessing them at once, neither delivered he them into the hand of Joshua.

JUDGES iii. 1, 2

Now these are the peoples which Yahweh left, to prove Israel by them (even as many as had not known the wars of Canaan—only that the generations of the children of Israel might know), to teach them war, at the least such as beforetime knew nothing thereof.

JUDGES iii. 5, 6

So the children of Israel dwelt among the Canaanites— and they took of their daughters to be their wives, and gave them their own daughters to their sons, and served their gods.

II

THE MATRIARCHATE

The question whether the matriarchate preceded the formation of the family (polygamous or monogamous) among primitive peoples generally is a larger question than we care to discuss in this volume. We can only refer to the works of such anthropologists or sociologists as have given special attention to this perplexing problem. Says A. H. Keane, in his recent volume, *Man, Past and Present*, p. 6 f: " In the clan system descent was probably reckoned at first only through the female line ; consequently uterine ties alone constituted kinship—the father not being considered related to his own children or a member of the family." But in other passages this same student admits that the contrary may have been true ; he even suggests that the problem belongs to the sociologists rather than to his own peculiar province, that of anthropology.

When, however, we pass to Semitic peoples we find the weight of evidence is in favour of the matriarchate as the primitive form of society. The data presented by W. Robertson Smith in his *Kinship and Marriage*, point this way ; though the said data, it must be admitted, are far from being primitive data. More conclusive are certain facts that appear in the ancient Hebrew sources. The *sadiqa* marriages, marriages in which women remained with their clan and reared children thereto, must not be overlooked. Then there is the fact that the harlot in ancient Israel, as among other Semitic peoples, had some social position which points in the same direction. The persistence of old customs among such a people is generally recognised. The harlot having a tent or home of her own into which she received her lovers without incurring the disfavour of her clan, was a survival of the age of the matriarchate. Such women as Rahab and Delilah are mentioned naturally as a legitimate part of the social life of their people. And

.what was characteristic of the Canaanites here appears to have been true of the Hebrews themselves. Even at a much later day certain of the patriarchs are mentioned as going in to harlots with no suggestion that they incurred the disfavour of the social body of which they were a part by doing so.

III

THE PHILISTINES

According to Amos ix. 7 the Philistines came from Caphtor (cf. Deut. ii. 23), *i.e.*, as is now supposed Crete. In the time of Rameses III., the Pursta, or Pulsta (the Philistines), made their way into Northern Egypt, only to be repulsed and turned up the seaboard of Western Palestine. That they seem to have emigrated from the south appears from the fact that all but one (Askalon) of their cities were on the great highways. That they entered the land of Canaan from the southwest about the time the Hebrews entered from the east is thought probable. Because they were not great in point of numbers they were slow in getting the territory, which they are known to have occupied in the days of Saul, into their hands. This accounts also for their letting Israel alone until near the close of the period of the Judges. The Tell-el-Amarna letters or tablets have no mention of them. This accords with what we have already noted. If they slowly spread out, incorporating many of the Canaanites, as seems probable, they were ready to give Israel trouble at the close of the days of the Judges. Their slow progress may have been owing to their being harried occasionally by Egypt. George Adam Smith thinks they were a Semitic people. That they became partly Semitised through contact with the Canaanites and other Semites is probable; but that they belonged originally to the Aryan stock is also probable. A large number of Semitic words among their proper names does not prove more than this. They reached the height of their power in the time of Saul, and did much to increase the perplexity in which he passed his years. The hegemony of Ephraim was broken by them, it is thought, in the battle of Ebenezer, as later Israel was overwhelmed at Mount Gilboa. At the time of Saul's death David held Ziklag as a vassal of the Philistines. While this monarch ruled at Hebron he was not strong enough to cope with these enemies, but after the union of the tribes he quickly humbled them. The Philistines were never strong enough to cope successfully with a united Israel. (See *Encyclopædia Britannica*, vol. xviii., pp. 174 f., 755 ff.; xiii., p. 402 ; xxi., p. 645 ; Dillmann, *Genesis*, vol. i., p. 361 f. ; Cornill, *History of the People of Israel*, p. 45 ; George Adam Smith, *Historical Geog. of the Holy Land*, etc.)

IV

THE HITTITES (THE KHITTIM)

Anciently there dwelt to the north of Syria, between the Orontes and the Euphrates, a powerful, warlike people, known to the Assyrians as the Khatti, to the Hebrews as the Khittim, to the Egyptians as the Khita. That a branch of this people existed in the south of Palestine long prior to the days of the settlement by the Hebrews may be deemed possible but not probable. Such references as Gen. xv. 20 are now regarded suspiciously by scholars. Though Palestine was undoubtedly oft traversed by the Khittim, it was not, we may safely conclude, or at least surmise, colonised by them. The Khittim, mentioned as early as the sixteenth century, appear to have been powerful as late as the twelfth century. The hostile relations which existed between them and the Assyrians account for the frequent mention of them by the latter. They were not Semites; they appear to have been of rougher, sturdier, northern stock. With Egypt they were often on unfriendly terms. But when Rameses II. obtained over them at great cost a victory, peace was brought about, and the marriage of the daughter of the King of the Khittim to Rameses cemented the new friendly league. There is nothing to suggest that the Khittim played any part in Canaan during the days of the Judges. Their relations with Egypt seem to have been such as to forbid it. (See *Encyc. Brit.*, vol. xii., p. 25 ff.; vol. xxii., p. 822; Hastings' *Dictionary*, vol. ii., p. 390 ff.; Dillmann, *Genesis*, vol. i., p. 363 f.; and C. R. Conder, *The Hittites*. This last work, which ought to be our leading authority on the Khittim, etc., should be very cautiously used.)

V

THE AMORITES

In the E and D documents of the Hexateuch the term " Amorites " appears to be the common one in use to designate the pre-Israelitish inhabitants of the land of Canaan, in the territory west of the Jordan; yet even in these documents the term " Canaanites " is made frequent use of in speaking of the inhabitants of the lowlands along the seaboard. Frequently, it is true, the Amorites are spoken of as the people ruled by Sihon and Og east of the Jordan. In the J document the familiar designation of the pre-Israelitish inhabitants of Canaan is " Canaanites." Driver, in his commentary on Deuteronomy, concludes that so far as can be judged from the biblical and other data at present at our disposal, that Canaan, before it came into the possession of the Israelites, must have been occupied principally by two tribes—the Amorites and the Canaanites— each sufficiently numerous and prominent to supply a designation of the entire country; the former, it may be inferred, resident chiefly in the high central ground of Palestine, and the latter chiefly in the lower districts on the west and east. From a survey of the passages quoted, it appears, further, that, as Wellhausen remarks, while the Canaanites are often alluded to as still resident in the land in the age of the biblical writer especially in the cities of

the plains not conquered by the Israelites, the Amorites
are usually referred to as the past population of Canaan,
expelled by the Israelites, and as such are invested with
semi-mythical attributes, and described as giants. This is
putting it quite as strongly as the facts now known warrant us in doing, for even Amos (ii. 9 f.) uses the term
"Amorites," as does E, as a general term for the primitive
population of Canaan. Winckler thinks that according to
the Amarna letters the Canaanite inhabitants were in the
coasts and the Amorites in the interior. While we may
admit this, which accords substantially with the thought
of Driver and Wellhausen, we may also contend that the
Canaanites probably, though distinct from the Amorites,
crowded up in the richer regions among the hills. That
there was a people known as Amorites seems unquestionable ; but that they were often confounded by late narrators with the Canaanites seems also unquestionable. (See
Encyc. Brit., vol. i., p. 747 ; vol. iv., p. 763 ; vol. xiii., p.
397 ; vol. xvi., p. 533 ; Driver, *Deuteronomy*, p. 11 f.;
Cheyne and Black, *Encyc. Bib.*, vol. i., c. 146 f.; Hastings'
Dictionary, vol. i., p. 84 ff.)

VI

THE SPIRIT OF YAHWEH

The phrase "spirit of Yahweh" often appeared in the
literature of this period. It must have been with even
greater frequency upon the tongues of the people, for all
men who accomplished deeds of unusual prowess, or who
manifested peculiar skill in the arts, were thought of as
possessed by this spirit. He who was seized by it was in
a sort of demonic fury, a divine rage. Unusual enthusiasm, such as would enable a man to rise above his ordinary
level of performance, was enough to suggest it. Whatever
seemed to transcend the limits of man's own sagacity and
strength was attributed, says G. F. Moore, "to the energy

of the spirit of Yahweh, the genius of the artist, the inspiration of the poet, the frenzy of the prophets and their revelations, and extraordinary feats of any kind.'' This spirit came upon Gideon (Judges vi. 34), upon Jephthah (Judges xi. 29), upon Samson (Judges xiii. 25 ; xiv. 6, 19 ; xv. 14), upon Saul (1 Samuel x. 10 ; xi. 6, etc.). (See Kautzsch, *Literature of the Old Testament*, p. 23 ; Moore, *Judges, I. C.*, pp. 87 f., 197, 298 ; H. P. Smith, *Samuel, I. C.*, pp. 68, 145.)

VII

THE PATRIARCHAL STORIES OF GENESIS

It is somewhat aside from the main purpose of this volume to discuss the larger question of the historicity of Genesis, or the lesser one of the character of the patriarchal narratives. There is considerable difference of opinion among scholars, some still accepting as probable a considerable basis of fact in these stories, others, and the number seems to be increasing, holding the contrary view. The following statement by Budde, *The Religion of Israel to the Exile*, will meet with hearty response on the part of many : ''For the patriarchs are, in reality, nothing more than the ideal reflection of the nation Israel thrown back into the past—Israel as it should have been in hoary antiquity. No nation knows the actual father from whom it takes its origin ; for nations never arise by derivation from the same father, but by the aggregation of clans and tribes. The realisation of these facts, to be sure, deprives the whole story of the patriarchs of historicity in the narrower sense, but not of historical value, still less of inner worth and psychological truth.''

One thing which we should not overlook is the fact that the literature of the period we considered in Part I. of this volume, a literature covering two and a half or three centuries, which consists of portions of Joshua, and most of Judges and 1 Samuel, contains even in its present form only

two passages in which the patriarchs are mentioned—Josh.
xxiv. 2, 3, 4, 32, and 1 Sam. xii. 8. The latter passage may
be dismissed as it refers to Jacob as a people, a term used
frequently in the later literature much as the term Israel
appears to have been. The verses in Joshua xxiv. read as
follows : '' And Joshua said unto all the people, Thus
saith the Lord, the God of Israel, Your fathers dwelt of old
time beyond the River, even Terah, the father of Abraham,
and the father of Nahor : and they served other gods.
And I took your father Abraham from beyond the River,
and led him throughout all the land of Canaan, and multiplied his seed, and gave him Isaac. And I gave unto
Isaac Jacob and Esau : and I gave unto Esau Mount Seir,
to possess it ; and Jacob and his children went down into
Egypt. . . . And the bones of Joseph, which the children
of Israel brought up out of Egypt, buried they in Shechem,
in the parcel of ground which Jacob bought of the sons of
Hamor the father of Shechem, for an hundred pieces of
money : and they became the inheritance of the children of
Joseph.'' But this chapter belongs unquestionably not to
the contemporary literature, but to a late narrator, probably E, or a redactor of E, who reminds us of the Deuteronomists. For historical purposes it is well nigh worthless. It is significant that in the folk-stories and songs of
these centuries, so far as they have come down to us, we
have no mention of any patriarchs. The only reasonable
conclusion is that there were no such men known to the
Hebrew clans of the time. To the centuries back of their
Egyptian sojourn they were unable to go in thought.

Premising, then, that there were none, because the contemporary literature is silent, we go farther and note how
such stories as those which have to do with Abraham and
other of the patriarchs sprang up in Israel during the monarchy. As the Hebrews endeavoured to idealise their past,
to tell the story of their servitude in Egypt, or of their con-
flicts and their covenants with the Philistines, and especially as their reformers set themselves to purify the old

Canaanitish sanctuaries of the lewd worship of the Baalim, they made use of this form of literature. Take, for example, the latter case. By representing their supposed progenitors as journeying through Canaan, as building altars, and worshipping Yahweh at Bethel, Beersheba, etc., they could hallow these old sanctuaries in the eyes of the people. It was not, we need to remember, until the law of Deuteronomy, promulgated in the days of Josiah, discredited these high places that any determined effort was made to abolish them. Pre-Deuteronomic reformers at the most sought only to purify them. So admirably has Professor B. W. Bacon, in an article on *Abraham, the Heir of Yahweh*, done his work that it is enough here to call attention to it.[1]

VIII

PRIMITIVE COVENANTS AMONG SEMITIC PEOPLE

"The very idea of a 'covenant' in primitive thought," says Henry Clay Trumbull, D.D., in one of his three valuable works on the subject, "is a union of being, or of persons, in a common life, with the approval of God, or the gods. This was primarily a sharing of blood, which is life, between two persons, through a rite which had the sanction of him who is the source of all life. In this sense 'blood brotherhood' and the 'threshold covenant' are but different forms of one and the same *covenant*. The blood of animals shared in a common sacrifice is counted as the blood which makes two one in a sacred covenant. Wine as 'the blood of the grape' stands for the blood which is the life of all flesh; hence the sharing of wine stands for the sharing of blood or life. So, again, salt represents

[1] *The New World*, vol. viii., p. 674 ff. ; cf., however, the article on *Abraham*, Cheyne and Black, *Encyc. Bib.* (T. K. C.), vol. i., c. 23 ff.

blood, or life, and the covenant of salt is simply another
form of the one blood covenant." Equally worthy of note
are his words concerning marriage as a covenant : "True
marriage is thus a covenant, instead of an arrangement.
The twain become no longer two, but one ; each is given
to the other ; their separate identity is lost in their common life. A ring, a bracelet, a band, has been from time
immemorial the symbol and pledge of such an indissoluble
union."

There are occasional references in the period under consideration to covenants between individuals, as that between Jonathan and David (1 Sam. xviii. 2 and xxii. 16 ff.)
and that at the beginning of the period of the monarchy
between Abner and David (2 Samuel iii. 12 ff.). It is possible that the very frequency of such covenants between individuals may in part account for the mention of so few.
Most of the stories of early covenants in the Old Testament, in which individuals figure prominently, were in
reality covenants between peoples, as in Gen. xxvi. 26 ff. the
covenant was between Israel and the Philistines. This is
according to J. The similar story, in Gen. xxi. 22 ff. is in
the E document of the Hexateuch. So in the narrative of
the covenant between Jacob and Laban, Gen. xxxi. 44 ff.,
where a cairn was reared as a witness and landmark, the
covenant was in fact between the Hebrews and the Ara-
mæans. According to Ex. xxiii. 32 (cf. Ex. xxxiv. 10-17) in
the Book of the Covenant, which was posterior to the time
of the Judges, the Hebrews were told not to make a covenant with the Canaanites. But that they repeatedly covenanted with them as they settled the land, and during
the immediately following centuries, cannot reasonably be
doubted,

INDEX

For Product Safety Concerns and Information please contact our EU
representative GPSR@taylorandfrancis.com
Taylor & Francis Verlag GmbH, Kaufingerstraße 24, 80331 München, Germany

www.ingramcontent.com/pod-product-compliance
Lightning Source LLC
Chambersburg PA
CBHW070356270326
41926CB00014B/2566